LONDON
QUIZ

LONDON QUIZ

How well do you know London?

Travis Elborough and
Nick Rennison

THE LITTLE BOOKROOM • NEW YORK

© 2010 The Little Bookroom

Text © 2010 Travis Elborough and Nick Rennison
Based on a design by Sarah Caplan / MPH Design

Map on cover and throughout designed by Kerry Lee,
Published by Pictorial Maps Ltd, Printed by Chromoworks Ltd. in Great Britain.
Every attempt has been made to contact, obtain permission from, and properly
acknowledge copyright holder. Please contact the publisher
and corrections will be made in future editions.

Library of Congress Cataloging-in-Publication Data

Elborough, Travis.
London quiz / by Travis Elborough and Nick Rennison.
p. cm.
ISBN 978-1-892145-87-1 (alk. paper)
1. London (England)--Miscellanea. I. Rennison, Nick, 1955- II. Title.
DA677.E45 2011
942.1--dc22   2010014405

Published by The Little Bookroom
435 Hudson Street, Suite 300, New York, NY 10014
editorial@littlebookroom.com
www.littlebookroom.com

Printed in the United States of America

2 4 6 8 0 9 7 5 3 1

CONTENTS

Introduction 7

INTRODUCTION

London is full of stories, curiosities and echoes of its past and one of the best ways to unearth them is to ask questions. The questions in this quiz book are not meant to be easy. Indeed, many of them are very difficult. However, the questions and their answers are very definitely intended to be interesting and to provide entry points to the fascinating history of the city. In a series of themed sections from Crime and Punishment and London in the Movies to London Firsts and The London Dead, we have posed 400 questions, each of which has three possible answers. The result, we hope, is a quiz book that is entertaining and intriguing.

Crime & Punishment

1. **For what is the eighteenth-century thief Jack Sheppard best remembered?**

   ☐ a. His escapes from prison
   ☐ b. He robbed Sir Robert Walpole, the prime minister
   ☐ c. He was the subject of a poem by Alexander Pope

2. **Why was a Frenchman named Robert Hubert hanged at Tyburn in 1666?**

   ☐ a. He had attempted to assassinate Charles II
   ☐ b. He had confessed to starting the Great Fire of London
   ☐ c. He had confessed to being a spy for Louis XIV of France

3. **What was the main aim of the Cato Street conspirators, a group of radical revolutionaries captured by Bow Street Runners in a stable loft in Cato Street, off the Edgware Road, in February 1820?**

   ☐ a. To murder the Prime Minister and the Cabinet as they dined at a house in Grosvenor Square
   ☐ b. To assassinate the Prince Regent as he travelled in a coach along Oxford Street
   ☐ c. To kidnap and hold for ransom Princess Victoria, the baby daughter of the Duke of Kent and future queen

4. **What happened to the body of William Duell after he was hanged at Tyburn on 24th November 1740?**

   ☐ a. It was stolen by 'resurrection men'
   ☐ b. It began to breathe again while being prepared for dissection
   ☐ c. It was mummified and placed on display at Surgeons' Hall in Cloth Fair

5. **Where was the pirate Captain Kidd executed in 1701?**

   ☐ a. Tyburn
   ☐ b. Tower Hall
   ☐ c. Execution Dock

6. **How did the serial killer John George Haigh dispose of the body of his first victim in his workshop at 79, Gloucester Road, SW7 in September 1944?**

   ☐ a. He dissolved it in a bath of acid
   ☐ b. He cut it up and left it in several parcels in Gloucester Road tube station
   ☐ c. He threw it into the Thames near Waterloo Bridge

7. **What happened in December 1867 at the Clerkenwell House of Detention, which used to stand on the site of the Royal Mail's sorting office at Mount Pleasant, EC1?**

   ☐ a. Fifteen men tunnelled out of the building in a mass escape
   ☐ b. A bomb exploded and twelve people were killed
   ☐ c. The last public execution took place outside its gate

8. **What crime is commemorated by a plaque in Maiden Lane, WC2?**

   ☐ a. The assassination of Sir Henry Wilson in 1922
   ☐ b. The murder of the actor William Terriss in 1897
   ☐ c. The shooting of the racing driver David Blakely in 1955

9. **What happened to John and Sheila Matthews at their home in Balcombe Street, NW1, on 6 December 1975?**

    ☐ a. They were shot by a deranged sniper in a block of flats opposite their building
    ☐ b. They were killed by a cat burglar whom they surprised in the act of stealing Mrs. Matthews' jewellery
    ☐ c. They were taken hostage by IRA gunmen

10. **Which famous playwright killed an actor in a duel in Hoxton in 1598?**

    ☐ a. Christopher Marlowe
    ☐ b. William Shakespeare
    ☐ c. Ben Jonson

11. **Where was Spencer Perceval when he became the only British Prime Minister to be assassinated?**

    ☐ a. On the staircase in 10 Downing Street
    ☐ b. In the lobby of the House of Commons
    ☐ c. Outside his house in Lincoln's Inn Fields

12. **Who were Elizabeth Stride and Catherine Eddowes?**

    ☐ a. Two female pirates
    ☐ b. Two famous prostitutes in eighteenth-century Covent Garden
    ☐ c. Two of the victims of Jack the Ripper

13. **Which infamous murderer is associated with Hilldrop Crescent in Camden?**

    ☐ a. Dr. Crippen
    ☐ b. Jack the Ripper
    ☐ c. John Reginald Christie

14. **For what 'crime' was the poet Leigh Hunt imprisoned in the Horsemonger Lane gaol in 1813?**

    ☐ a. Defacing Westminster Bridge
    ☐ b. Insulting the Prince Regent
    ☐ c. Impersonating a Chelsea Pensioner

15. **Whose body was found on Greenberry Hill after he had allegedly been murdered by three men named Green, Berry and Hill?**

    ☐ a. Sir Edmund Godfrey, a seventeenth-century magistrate involved in the Popish Plot
    ☐ b. Sir Godfrey Edmunds, an eighteenth-century judge who had sentenced to death several of the Gordon Rioters
    ☐ c. Sir Edward Geoffreys, a nineteenth-century judge who had sentenced several early trade unionists to transportation to Australia

16. **In London history, what was Evil May Day?**

    ☐ a. A day of riots against foreigners in the city in 1517
    ☐ b. The day on which the deaths of the first plague victims were recorded in 1665
    ☐ c. The day on which the Houses of Parliament burned to the ground in 1834

17. **What happened at the execution of convicted murderers Owen Haggerty and John Holloway outside Newgate prison on 22 February 1807?**

☐ a. Friends of the prisoners stormed the gallows and staged a last-minute rescue of the condemned men

☐ b. A panic started in the crowd and more than thirty people were trampled to death

☐ c. The trapdoors on the gallows failed to open and the men could not be hung

18. **How did the actress and singer Martha Ray meet her death outside what is now the Royal Opera House on 7 April 1779?**

☐ a. She was hung from a lamppost by a rioting mob of theatregoers

☐ b. She was shot by a clergyman

☐ c. She was stabbed in the heart by a Bow Street Runner

19. **What was the so-called Pimlico Mystery of 1886?**

☐ a. The death by chloroform poisoning of a grocer named Thomas Edwin Bartlett

☐ b. The death by arsenic poisoning of a music hall comedian named Albert Edward Ricardo

☐ c. The sudden disappearance from her home of a dressmaker named Mary Jane Craddock

20. **How was Richard Rose executed at Smithfield in 1532?**

☐ a. Boiled alive

☐ b. Burned alive

☐ c. Flayed alive

LONDON QUIZ

London in the Movies

1. **Where do Withnail and I smoke a Camberwell Carrot in the 1986 film of that name?**

   ☐ a. Camden
   ☐ b. Camberwell
   ☐ c. Crouch End

2. **William Friese-Greene is credited with producing the first moving pictures on celluloid film in a London park. Which one?**

   ☐ a. Regent's Park
   ☐ b. St. James's Park
   ☐ c. Hyde Park

3. **In the 1949 Ealing Studio comedy *Passport to Pimlico*, bomb damage uncovers ancient documents that reveal that the London district in the title belongs to which foreign dynasty?**

   ☐ a. The Duchy of Burgundy
   ☐ b. The Elector of Saxony
   ☐ c. The King of Redonda

4. **For several years the derelict gas works at Beckton in East London provided a versatile canvas for moviemakers looking to recreate far more exotic locations. Which of the following places did Beckton not stand in for?**

   ☐ a. The jungles of Vietnam
   ☐ b. A Japanese internment camp in China
   ☐ c. The bridge over the River Kwai

5. **What happens to the River Thames in the British science fiction classic *The Day the Earth Caught Fire*?**

   ☐ a. It rises to flood the whole of London
   ☐ b. It runs dry
   ☐ c. It becomes radioactive and bursts into flames

6. **In *An American Werewolf in London*, where does the lycanthropic David awake to find himself naked?**

   ☐ a. London Zoo
   ☐ b. Selfridges Food Hall
   ☐ c. The Isle of Dogs

7. **The Planet Hollywood restaurant in Piccadilly appears in which British romantic comedy?**

   ☐ a. *Four Weddings and a Funeral*
   ☐ b. *Bridget Jones' Diary*
   ☐ c. *About a Boy*

8. **Why might Arsenal fans be up in arms over the film *Fever Pitch*?**

   ☐ a. The north London club are shown being thrashed 6-0 by local rivals Tottenham Hotspur
   ☐ b. Manchester United boss Alex Ferguson has a cameo role playing the team's manager
   ☐ c. Craven Cottage, home to Fulham, is substituted for Arsenal's old Highbury Stadium

9. **In the noir classic *Night and the City* where does the two-bit hustler Harry Fabian meet his end?**

   ☐ a. On the steps of St. Paul's Cathedral
   ☐ b. By Hammersmith Bridge
   ☐ c. In a Soho back alley

10. Where exactly was hell in Clive Barker's 1980s blood-curdler *Hellraiser*?

☐ a. Dulwich
☐ b. Dalston
☐ c. Dollis Hill

11. What according to Billy Fisher, the daydreaming Northerner in John Schlesinger's *Billy Liar*, can a man do in London?

☐ a. Lose his virginity
☐ b. Lose his mind
☐ c. Lose himself

12. Who narrated Patrick Keiller's film *London*?

☐ a. Paul Schofield
☐ b. Paul Darrow
☐ c. Paul Eddington

13. Of what did James Mason give filmgoers a tour in 1967?

☐ a. London in the Raw
☐ b. The London That Nobody Knows
☐ c. The London Dickens Knew

14. Which of Woody Allen's so-called London trilogy was never granted a cinema release in the capital?

☐ a. *Match Point*
☐ b. *Cassandra's Dream*
☐ c. *Scoop*

15. **A substantial part of the plot of Hanif Kureishi's *London Kills Me* concerns a hunt around Notting Hill for what?**

    ☐ a. A pair of shoes
    ☐ b. A decent burger
    ☐ c. A hitman

16. **Which London station provides the backdrop to the 1955 Ealing comedy *The Ladykillers*?**

    ☐ a. Marylebone
    ☐ b. Fenchurch Street
    ☐ c. St. Pancras

17. **What number London bus does Cliff Richard drive across Europe in the full-colour film musical *Summer Holiday*?**

    ☐ a. 9 to Piccadilly
    ☐ b. 35 to Clapham
    ☐ c. 8 to Bow

18. **What street did the director Michael Powell (who used it to sinister effect in his film *Peeping Tom*) describe as 'a narrow, arched passageway that gives you goose bumps just to look at it'?**

    ☐ a. Craven Passage, Covent Garden
    ☐ b. Newman Passage, Fitzrovia
    ☐ c. Artillery Passage, Spitalfields

19. **In the Richard Curtis comedy *Notting Hill*, the character played by Hugh Grant is the owner of what kind of business?**

    ☐ a. An antiques stall on the Portobello Road Market
    ☐ b. A bookshop on the Portobello Road
    ☐ c. A secondhand record shop on the Portobello Road

20. Wardour Street has been the administrative home of the British movie industry since the 1920s. Which once illustrious film company had offices at 113 Wardour Street?

☐ a. London Films
☐ b. Hammer Films
☐ c. British Lion

1. **Ronnie Scott first opened the legendary jazz club that continues to bear his name on 30 October 1959. What instrument did Scott himself play?**

   ☐ a. Clarinet
   ☐ b. Trumpet
   ☐ c. Tenor sax

2. **A statue of which famous composer stands in Ebury Street, close to where he once lived?**

   ☐ a. Mozart as a child
   ☐ b. Paganini with a violin with broken strings
   ☐ c. Mendelssohn with a conductor's baton in his hand

3. **What London landmark can be spotted on the record sleeve of Wings' 'London Town'?**

   ☐ a. Big Ben
   ☐ b. Tower Bridge
   ☐ c. The Tower of London

4. **The 2 I's coffee bar on Old Compton Street is often called the birthplace of British rock 'n' roll and its cellar was the venue for early performances by Cliff Richard, Tommy Steele and Vince Taylor. What did the 'I' stand for?**

   ☐ a. Iranians
   ☐ b. Italians
   ☐ c. Intellectuals

5. **Two very different musicians both have blue plaques to their names in adjoining houses in Brook Street. Who are they?**

   ☐ a. Duke Ellington and Wolfgang Amadeus Mozart
   ☐ b. Jimi Hendrix and George Frederick Handel
   ☐ c. Noel Coward and Edward Elgar

6. **To what does the title of Gustav Holst's *St. Paul's Suite* refer?**

   ☐ a. St. Paul's Cathedral where he had been a chorister as a child
   ☐ b. St. Paul's Girls' School in Hammersmith where he was director of music
   ☐ c. St. Paul's Church in Wilton Place where he was organist

7. **What was the punk rock pioneer Ian Dury's first group called?**

   ☐ a. Balham and the B-Roads
   ☐ b. The Clapham Junction Stranglers
   ☐ c. Kilburn and the High Roads

8. **Joe Meek, the record producer behind Telstar, recorded many of his greatest hits above a store at 304 Holloway Road. What did it sell?**

   ☐ a. Soft furnishings
   ☐ b. Leather goods
   ☐ c. Automotive spare parts

9. **Tower House, 29 Melbury Road, Kensington, the turreted Gothic pile built by William Burges in 1877, was home to which guitar god nearly a century later?**

   ☐ a. Jimmy Page
   ☐ b. Eric Clapton
   ☐ c. Ritchie Blackmore

10. **Where in London did Mick Jagger pen the lyrics to his call-to-arms anthem 'Street Fighting Man'?**

    ☐ a. Outside the US Embassy in Grosvenor Square during an anti-Vietnam War rally

    ☐ b. On the top deck of a Number 19 bus on the way to the Regent Sound studio on Denmark Street

    ☐ c. At 48 Cheyne Walk, his 1711 Queen Anne town house in Chelsea

11. **What did Ray Davies of the Kinks nearly call 'Waterloo Sunset'?**

    ☐ a. Muswell Hill Daybreak

    ☐ b. Waterloo Sunrise

    ☐ c. Liverpool Sunset

12. **On what occasion did Bob Dylan, making his first visit to London in 1962, perform 'Masters of War' and 'Hollis Brown' at the Pindar of Wakefield Singer's Club in King's Cross?**

    ☐ a. A Christmas party

    ☐ b. Ewan Macoll and Peggy Seeger's engagement party

    ☐ c. A party celebrating the 10th anniversary of Queen Elizabeth II's coronation

13. **Which of the following is a piece of classical music by the Australian composer Percy Grainger?**

    ☐ a. Brahms in Bloomsbury

    ☐ b. Handel in the Strand

    ☐ c. Mozart in Mayfair

14. **According to the lyrics of George and Ira Gershwin's 'A Foggy Day (In London Town)', what has lost its charm?**

   ☐ a. The River Thames
   ☐ b. The Houses of Parliament
   ☐ c. The British Museum

15. **Why was Hector Berlioz staying in London in Queen Anne Street in the year 1851?**

   ☐ a He was conducting a performance of his own *Symphonie Fantastique*
   ☐ b. He was the French judge of musical instruments at the Great Exhibition
   ☐ c. He was in pursuit of the English actress Harriet Smithson with whom he had fallen in love

16. **Where were the London headquarters of The Beatles' Apple Corp?**

   ☐ a. 66 Carnaby Street
   ☐ b. 221B Baker Street
   ☐ c. 3 Savile Row

17. **What was unusual about the concert Chopin gave at the Guildhall on 16 November 1848?**

   ☐ a. It was the only one he ever gave in London
   ☐ b. It was the last public performance of his life
   ☐ c. He played the violin rather than the piano

18. **Before rock stardom beckoned what summer job did Rod Stewart have?**

   a. Abattoir assistant at Smithfield Market
   b. Morgue attendant in Muswell Hill
   c. Gravedigger in Highgate Cemetery

19. **Who opened HMV's first music store at 363 Oxford Street on 21 July 1921?**

   ☐ a. Edward Elgar
   ☐ b. Rin Tin Tin
   ☐ c. Enrico Caruso

20. **The song "The Lambeth Walk", from the hit musical *Me and My Girl* became such a phenomenon in the 1930s that it was:**

   ☐ a. Adopted by the BBC as their early morning theme tune
   ☐ b. Denounced by the Nazis as 'Jewish mischief and animalistic hopping'
   ☐ c. Performed at the last night of the Proms in 1939, after "Land of Hope and Glory"

Theatrical London

1. **At which London theatre did David Garrick make his stage debut?**

   ☐ a. The Curtain, Shoreditch
   ☐ b. The Lincoln's Inn Fields Theatre
   ☐ c. Goodman's Fields Theatre

2. **The Theatre, Shoreditch, opened by James Burbage in 1576, was one of London's earliest playhouses. It was taken down in 1598, but what happened to its timbers?**

   ☐ a. They were used to build The Globe on Bankside
   ☐ b. They were used to burn Burbage and his company of actors at the stake for heresy
   ☐ c. They were used in the construction of the warship *The Mary Rose*

3. **Where in London can you find a statue of Sir Henry Irving, the first actor to be knighted?**

   ☐ a. Shaftesbury Avenue
   ☐ b. Leicester Square
   ☐ c. Charing Cross Road

4. **In 1881 The Savoy Theatre opened on the Strand. It had been created by Richard D'Oyly Carte to stage Gilbert and Sullivan operas. What was it the first building in London to boast?**

   ☐ a. Electric lights
   ☐ b. A public address system
   ☐ c. Fitted carpets

5. **Which playwright was once a St. Pancras borough councillor?**

   ☐ a. Harold Pinter
   ☐ b. George Bernard Shaw
   ☐ c. Terence Rattigan

6. **At which London theatre was John Osborne's *Look Back in Anger* first staged?**

   ☐ a. The Young Vic, The Cut
   ☐ b. The Bush Theatre, Shepherd's Bush Green
   ☐ c. The Royal Court, Sloane Square

7. **When the London Coliseum, now home to the English National Opera company, opened in 1904, what special service was it rumoured to have laid on for Edward VII and his guests?**

   ☐ a. The armrests in their seats were fitted with gold plated taps that dispensed champagne throughout the performance
   ☐ b. There was a train that conveyed the King and his entourage from the entrance hall to the Royal Box
   ☐ c. A baccarat table was set up in the Royal Box, so the King didn't have to bother watching the play

8. **The presence of what hampered the expansion of Collins' Music Hall in Islington when it was rebuilt in 1897?**

   ☐ a. A burial ground
   ☐ b. Quicksand
   ☐ c. The low-lying roof of a tunnel on the Northern Line

9. **The royalties from which play, first performed at the Duke of York Theatre in Drury Lane in 1904, were donated to Great Ormond Street Hospital?**

   ☐ a. *Mary Poppins*
   ☐ b. *The Water Babies*
   ☐ c. *Peter Pan or The Boy Who Wouldn't Grow Up*

10. **In December 1984, *Les Miserables* began what would be an eighteen-year run at The Ambassador's Theatre in the West End, but from which London stage had it transferred?**

    ☐ a. The Almeida, Islington
    ☐ b. Stratford East
    ☐ c. The Barbican

11. **Noel Coward's first publicly-produced musical revue, *London Calling!*, debuted in 1923. Where was it first performed?**

    ☐ a. The London Palladium
    ☐ b. The Duke of York's Theatre
    ☐ c. The Vaudeville Theatre

12. **The audience at Covent Garden rioted in 1809. Why?**

    ☐ a. The theatre had caught fire and they were trying to escape
    ☐ b. A food fight, with rotten vegetables, had escalated
    ☐ c. The audience couldn't see the stage from the gallery

13. **In 1968, the Greater London Council proposed a redevelopment of Covent Garden which would have threatened the Adelphi and which other four theatres:**

    ☐ a. Vaudeville, Garrick, Duchess, Lyceum
    ☐ b. Garrick, Almeida, Duke of York's, Lyceum
    ☐ c. Duchess, Dominion, Ambassadors, Garrick

14. **Which London theatre was built on a difficult site that included an underground river?**

    ☐ a. Lyric Hammersmith
    ☐ b. Sadler's Wells
    ☐ c. The Garrick

15. **Which Underground station, built on the site of a former West End theatre, is said to be haunted by the ghost of an actress?**

   ☐ a.   Covent Garden
   ☐ b.   Holborn
   ☐ c.   Aldwych

16. **What were the first two theatres in London to reopen after the Restoration of Charles II in 1660?**

   ☐ a.   Theatre Royal, Drury Lane and Lincoln's Inn Fields
   ☐ b.   Theatre Royal, Haymarket and the Garrick Theatre
   ☐ c.   Theatre Royal, Covent Garden and the Duchess Theatre

17. **Which London Theatre, known as a writers' theatre, led to the abolition of theatrical censorship in 1968?**

   ☐ a.   Soho Theatre
   ☐ b.   Royal Court Theatre
   ☐ c.   The Donmar Warehouse

18. **In 1973, the London production of the musical *Hair* was forced to close because part of which theatre's ceiling collapsed?**

   ☐ a.   The Palladium
   ☐ b.   The Shaftesbury
   ☐ c.   The Cambridge Theatre

19. **Which theatre was rebuilt with multi-tier ramps to accommodate *Starlight Express*, Andrew Lloyd Webber's musical on roller skates?**

- ☐ a. The Apollo Victoria
- ☐ b. The Piccadilly Theatre
- ☐ c. The Palace Theatre

20. **Beneath what theatre lurks one of London's most eccentric theatrical members' clubs, for actors, artists and miscellaneous creative types?**

- ☐ a. The Old Vic
- ☐ b. The Phoenix
- ☐ c. The Ambassadors Theatre

Royal London

1. **What does it signify if the Royal Standard is flying from the roof of Buckingham Palace?**

   ☐ a. That the Queen is in residence
   ☐ b. That a member of the Royal Family has died
   ☐ c. That the Palace is open to the public

2. **What is Queen Elizabeth (later the Queen Mother) reported to have said when Buckingham Palace was bombed during the Blitz?**

   ☐ a. 'There goes the West Wing'
   ☐ b. 'I hate these wretched Germans and their bombs'
   ☐ c. 'Now I can look the East End in the face'

3. **Which member of the Royal Family lived at Clarence House, The Mall, until 2002?**

   ☐ a. Prince Charles
   ☐ b. Prince William
   ☐ c. The Queen Mother

4. **From which King does King's Cross railway station derive its name?**

   ☐ a. Charles II
   ☐ b. George IV
   ☐ c. William IV

5. **What stood on the site of St. James's Palace in Pall Mall before Henry VIII built a new royal residence there in the 1530s?**

   ☐ a. A home for penitent prostitutes
   ☐ b. A leper hospital
   ☐ c. An abbey church

6. **The statue of which English queen stands outside St. Paul's Cathedral?**

   ☐ a. Queen Victoria
   ☐ b. Queen Elizabeth I
   ☐ c. Queen Anne

7. **What ill omen occurred at the coronation of Richard the Lionhearted in Westminster Abbey in September 1189?**

   ☐ a. The king lost one of his shoes
   ☐ b. The crown nearly fell off the king's head
   ☐ c. A bat swooped down towards the king's head as the crown was put on it

8. **Which royal memento can you see at the Wellcome Collection in the Euston Road?**

   ☐ a. A lock of George III's hair
   ☐ b. Queen Victoria's underwear
   ☐ c. Elizabeth I's purse

9. **Which Queen commissioned Inigo Jones to build the Queen's House at Greenwich?**

   ☐ a. Anne of Denmark
   ☐ b. Henrietta Maria
   ☐ c. Catherine of Braganza

10. **Who was the last reigning monarch to live at Kensington Palace?**

   ☐ a. George I
   ☐ b. George II
   ☐ c. George III

11. **The 124-foot Duke of York's Column stands in Waterloo Place just off the Mall and is topped by a statue of Prince Frederick, the second son of George III. When it was built, why did wits say the column was so high?**

☐ a. So that he could escape his creditors
☐ b. So that no one had to see his ugly face
☐ c. So that he could look down on the commoners beneath

12. **Which member of the Royal Family was born at 17 Bruton Street in Mayfair?**

☐ a. The Duke of Edinburgh
☐ b. The Queen
☐ c. Prince Michael of Kent

13. **The statue of Prince Albert on the Albert Memorial shows him holding a book in his hand. What book is it?**

☐ a. The Catalogue of the Great Exhibition
☐ b. The Bible
☐ c. The Complete Works of Shakespeare

14. **What role did members of the Dymoke family of Scrivelsby in Lincolnshire play at royal coronations from the fourteenth century to the nineteenth century?**

☐ a. They sat by the monarch's side in Westminster Abbey and reminded him or her of the coronation protocol
☐ b. They rode into Westminster Hall at the coronation banquet and challenged anyone to deny the right of the monarch to take the throne
☐ c. They rode as a guard in the monarch's carriage to and from the coronation

15. **Where in London can you find the only statue in Britain of George I?**

    ☐ a. In the crypt of St. Paul's Cathedral
    ☐ b. In the grounds of Buckingham Palace
    ☐ c. On top of the steeple of St. George's, Bloomsbury

16. **Napoleon III, the French emperor, lived in King Street before he came to his country's throne. What job did he undertake while he was in London?**

    ☐ a. He was a special constable in Trafalgar Square during the Chartist protests
    ☐ b. He was a journalist reporting on debates in the House of Commons
    ☐ c. He was a lawyer in a practice in Chancery Lane

17. **In 1689, why did William III choose to leave Whitehall Palace and take up residence instead at Kensington Palace?**

    ☐ a. There was a constant smell from blocked drains at Whitehall
    ☐ b. Whitehall was crowded and he hated to be surrounded by too many people
    ☐ c. The air in Whitehall made his asthma worse

18. **Which member of a royal family from outside Europe met William Gladstone in Downing Street in 1882?**

    ☐ a. King Thibaw of Burma
    ☐ b. The Zulu king Cetewayo
    ☐ c. Prempeh I, King of the Ashanti

19. **What caused the fire which destroyed most of Whitehall Palace in 1698?**

   ☐ a.   A washerwoman put her clothes on a brazier and they caught fire
   ☐ b.   A baker left his loaves in the royal ovens too long
   ☐ c.   A lady-in-waiting set the curtains in her room alight with a candle

20. **Which square, originally called King Square, has a statue of Charles II in it?**

   ☐ a.   Russell Square
   ☐ b.   Bedford Square
   ☐ c.   Soho Square

Folklore & Customs

LONDON QUIZ

1. **What sort of service takes place in Holy Trinity Church, Dalston, every February?**

   ☐ a. A Singers' Service in memory of Jenny Lind, the 'Swedish Nightingale' who sang regularly in Victorian London
   ☐ b. A Clowns' Service in memory of Joseph Grimaldi, the early nineteenth-century clown
   ☐ c. A Footballers' Service in memory of Herbert Chapman, the famous manager of Arsenal FC in the 1930s

2. **What is the Knollys Red Rose Rent?**

   ☐ a. A rose given to the Lord Mayor in payment of an ancient fine
   ☐ b. A rose given to the Queen in payment for land now covered by Bedford Square in Bloomsbury
   ☐ c. A rose given to the Worshipful Company of Mercers in payment for a property in Whitechapel

3. **Which legendary London bogeyman made his first appearance in print in a story of 1846 entitled *The String of Pearls*?**

   ☐ a. Sweeney Todd
   ☐ b. Spring-Heeled Jack
   ☐ c. The Highgate Vampire

4. **Why was the land at the back of what is now the British Museum once known as the Field of the Forty Footsteps?**

    ☐ a. The ghost of a nun was said to haunt it and leave her footsteps behind her
    ☐ b. Two brothers once fought a duel there and their footsteps could be seen on the grass for many years afterwards
    ☐ c. Footsteps were said to appear there at midnight on All Saints' Day every year

5. **Where in London does the Ceremony of the Keys take place every night?**

    ☐ a. The Houses of Parliament
    ☐ b. Buckingham Palace
    ☐ c. The Tower of London

6. **Who supposedly lies buried beneath one of the platforms at King's Cross railway station?**

    ☐ a. King Alfred the Great
    ☐ b. Boudicca
    ☐ c. Old King Cole

7. **What is the Pancake Greaze?**

    ☐ a. A pub in Soho
    ☐ b. A game played every Shrove Tuesday in Westminster School
    ☐ c. A type of theatrical makeup used at the Old Vic theatre

8. **According to legend, what happened during a performance of Marlowe's *Doctor Faustus* in the courtyard of the Belle Sauvage Inn on Ludgate Hill in 1588?**

   ☐ a. The actor playing Faustus disappeared and was never seen again
   ☐ b. The devil appeared on stage
   ☐ c. Two members of the audience died of fright

9. **Why do the Provosts of Eton and King's College, Cambridge place lilies and white roses each year on a spot in the Wakefield Tower in the Tower of London?**

   ☐ a. To commemorate a journey from Cambridge to London by Richard of Malmesbury, first Provost of both Eton and King's College
   ☐ b. To mark the saint's day of St. Thomas Becket who left money in his will for the building of all three places—Eton, King's College and the Wakefield Tower
   ☐ c. To honour Henry VI, the founder of Eton and King's College, Cambridge, who met his death in the Tower

10. **Who shares with the Crown the ownership of the swans on the Thames?**

    ☐ a. The Honourable Artillery Company
    ☐ b. The Dyers' and Vintners' Companies
    ☐ c. The Lord Mayor of London

11. **In the eighteenth century, which group of city workers was treated to an annual feast by a wealthy woman named Montagu?**

    ☐ a. Costermongers
    ☐ b. Watermen
    ☐ c. Chimney sweeps

12. **What happens on Good Friday in the churchyard of St. Bartholomew the Great in Smithfield?**

   ☐ a. Two teams play a no-holds-barred game of football that dates back to the Middle Ages
   ☐ b. Hot cross buns are left for poor widows of the parish on the tombstones
   ☐ c. A play about Pontius Pilate dating back to the fifteenth century is performed

13. **How is Billingsgate said to have got its name?**

   ☐ a. From a legendary king called Belinus
   ☐ b. From a minor Norse god called Billin
   ☐ c. From its traditional founder, a Saxon chief called Balin

14. **What is the Baddeley Cake?**

   ☐ a. A cake eaten every Twelfth Night in the green room of Drury Lane Theatre
   ☐ b. A cake baked every Easter Sunday in memory of an eighteenth-century Lord Mayor
   ☐ c. A cake eaten every Midsummer Day at a feast given by the Worshipful Company of Goldsmiths

15. **Where can a wooden cat named Kaspar be found at the dinner table?**

   ☐ a. Inner Temple Hall
   ☐ b. University College, London
   ☐ c. The Savoy Hotel

16. What form does the 'quit rent' take in the annual Quit Rent Ceremony at the Royal Courts of Justice?

☐ a. Six horseshoes and sixty-one nails
☐ b. Three pairs of gloves and a felt hat
☐ c. Two sides of bacon and a sirloin of beef

17. What are Doggett's Coat and Badge?

☐ a. Two items supposedly from the uniform of the first-ever Beefeater which are on display in the Tower of London
☐ b. Two of the belongings of the legendary founder of the Worshipful Company of Merchant Taylors which are on display in Merchant Taylors' Hall
☐ c. Two of the prizes given in an annual race on the Thames

18. What kind of ghost allegedly once haunted the streets of Ladbroke Grove?

☐ a. A phantom red bus
☐ b. A ghostly bear
☐ c. An Egyptian mummy

19. 19) The Peter Pan Cup is awarded to the victor in an annual London event. Which one?

☐ a. The London Marathon
☐ b. The Christmas swimming race in the Serpentine
☐ c. The Pancake Day races in Lincoln's Inn Fields

20. **What does the Lion Sermon, preached in the church of St. Katharine Cree every 16 October, commemorate?**

☐ a.   The safe return of Richard the Lionhearted from the Third Crusade

☐ b.   The rescue of a small child from a lion which had escaped from the King's Menagerie in the Tower of London

☐ c.   The deliverance of a seventeenth-century Lord Mayor from the jaws of a lion

Drinkers' London

1. **In 1446 The Hostellers of London were granted what?**

    ☐ a. Guild status
    ☐ b. The freedom to water their beer
    ☐ c. The right to sell beer

2. **What is the connection between Dirty Dicks pub opposite Liverpool Street Station in Bishopsgate and Charles Dickens?**

    ☐ a. The novelist's father drank himself to death there
    ☐ b. The pub's collection of stuffed cats inspired the novelist to write *The Old Curiosity Shop*
    ☐ c. Its namesake provided the basis for Miss Havisham in *Great Expectations*

3. **In the 1940s, why did the bohemian writers who haunted The Fitzroy Tavern on Charlotte Street dash en masse to the nearby Marquis of Granby at 10:30 pm every night?**

    ☐ a. It stayed open half an hour later
    ☐ b. The commissioning editors of the BBC went to the Marquis at that time each night
    ☐ c. Whatever sandwiches were left by then were given away free

4. **Victor Berlemont, the original French patron of The French House on Dean Street, was at one point reputedly the only foreign licensee in London. In honour of its Gallic heritage, this fine pub still refuses to serve what?**

    ☐ a. Anyone wearing an England shirt or scarf
    ☐ b. Pints
    ☐ c. Roast beef-flavoured crisps

5. **How did Major Alf Klein, the proprietor of the Duke of York between Charlotte Place and Rathbone Street, apparently initiate new male regulars to his pub?**
   - ☐ a. He made them drink a pint of slops
   - ☐ b. He forced them to arm wrestle him, barring them on the spot if they beat him
   - ☐ c. He cut the ends off their ties and hung them up behind the bar

6. **Norman Balon, the proprietor (known in the UK as a pub landlord) of the Coach and Horses in Soho for over sixty years, was celebrated as 'the rudest landlord in London'. Under what name did he often appear in the satirical magazine *Private Eye*?**
   - ☐ a. Bally Balon, the benign friend of the boozer
   - ☐ b. Monty Balon, the genial mine host
   - ☐ c. Norman Nice, the kindly landlord

7. **In 1888, the poet Francis Thompson was discovered lying intoxicated in the gutter outside which Soho pub by his future publisher Wilfred Meynell?**
   - ☐ a. The Crown and Two Chairmen, Dean Street
   - ☐ b. The Intrepid Fox, then on Wardour Street
   - ☐ c. The Pillars of Hercules, Greek Street

8. **Why is The Mitre Tavern in Ely Place in Holborn technically in Cambridgeshire?**

   ☐ a. Ely Place is among the lands belonging to the Bishop of Ely

   ☐ b. A former landlord, repenting of the dissolute life he'd led, donated the pub to the Abbey of Ely on his deathbed

   ☐ c. In 1547, the Major of Ely won the pub in a game of dice with its landlord

9. **Since 1820, what has a sailor done each Good Friday at the Widow's Son pub in Bow?**

   ☐ a. Rung the Bow Bell which is kept behind the bar

   ☐ b. Blown a candle out to commemorate the crucifixion

   ☐ c. Placed a hot cross bun in a basket hanging from the ceiling

10. **The Olde Wine Shades in Martin Lane near London Bridge is one of the only original pubs in the area to survive what?**

   ☐ a. The bombs of the Blitz in 1941

   ☐ b. The Great Fire of London in 1666

   ☐ c. The huge redevelopment of this part of London in the 1960s

11. **Who was caught at the Town of Ramsgate pub by Wapping Old Stairs, attempting to flee the country disguised as a sailor?**

   ☐ a. Judge Jeffreys

   ☐ b. King James II

   ☐ c. Oscar Wilde

12. **Whose ghost is said to haunt the Spaniard's Inn in Hampstead?**

    ☐ a. Dick Turpin
    ☐ b. Charles Dickens
    ☐ c. Dr. Johnson

13. **The toilets of which Victorian London pub are of such historical interest they are subject to a protection order?**

    ☐ a. The Princess Louise, High Holborn
    ☐ b. The Flask, Hampstead
    ☐ c. The Red Lion, St. James

14. **Why are the Fox and Anchor and New Market pubs in Smithfield at their busiest at 6 am in the morning?**

    ☐ a. They are favourites with all-night ravers leaving the nearby club Fabric
    ☐ b. It is a long-standing tradition that Fleet Street journalists read the first editions of that day's paper there
    ☐ c. They serve the porters and butchers clocking off from their night shifts at the nearby meat market

15. **Muriel Belcher was the founder and proprietress of which legendary Soho drinking den?**

    ☐ a. The Colony Room Club
    ☐ b. The Calamity Club
    ☐ c. The Casbah Club

16. **From which London tavern, demolished in the nineteenth century, did the pilgrims set out for Canterbury in Chaucer's tales?**

    ☐ a. The Tabard
    ☐ b. The Tankard
    ☐ c. The Table

17. **The Prospect of Whitby in Wapping is London's oldest remaining riverside inn. What was it originally named?**

    ☐ a. The Smuggler's Rest
    ☐ b. The Devil's Tavern
    ☐ c. The Damn Your Eyes

18. **The Rhymers Club, established by W. B. Yeats, met in which Fleet Street pub?**

    ☐ a. The Cheshire Cheese
    ☐ b. The Wine and Cheese
    ☐ c. The Cheese and Pickle

19. **From which pub did Samuel Pepys watch the Great Fire in 1666?**

    ☐ a. The Anchor
    ☐ b. The Coal Hole
    ☐ c. The Jerusalem Tavern

20. **Which 1960s group made their debut in the Clissold Arms on Fortes Green, Muswell Hill?**

    ☐ a. The Rolling Stones
    ☐ b. The Kinks
    ☐ c. The Small Faces

1. **How many London cinemas were destroyed during the war?**

   ☐ a. 10
   ☐ b. 30
   ☐ c. 60

2. **How were London Zoo's unfortunate manatees disposed of when the aquarium was deemed surplus to wartime requirements?**

   ☐ a. Eaten
   ☐ b. Shot
   ☐ c. Immolated in a dramatic fireball, seen on newsreels across the world

3. **According to a survey, what percentage of the capital's teenagers went to church each week during the war?**

   ☐ a. One
   ☐ b. Ten
   ☐ c. Fifty

4. **To what did the word 'doodlebug', the usual nickname for the Nazis' V1 rocket-powered drone bomb, originally refer?**

   ☐ a. A common insect
   ☐ b. A basic car
   ☐ c. An American railway carriage

5. **Which of the following jazz performers was not killed by enemy action during the war?**

   ☐ a. Al Bowlly
   ☐ b. Ken 'Snakehips' Johnson
   ☐ c. Harry Edgington

6. **For what wartime activity did Myra Hess gain her fame?**

   ☐ a. Lunchtime piano recitals in the National Gallery
   ☐ b. Singing popular songs broadcast from the BBC's studios in Lime Grove
   ☐ c. Dancing extracts from well-known ballets in Covent Garden

7. **For what was Covent Garden's Royal Opera House used during the war?**

   ☐ a. A vegetable store
   ☐ b. A dance hall
   ☐ c. A billet for GIs

8. **The U.S. Army's signal centre was based in an unused deep tunnel beneath which tube station?**

   ☐ a. Goodge Street
   ☐ b. Hampstead
   ☐ c. St. John's Wood

9. **Which television personality was born in 1944 in Highgate tube station?**

   ☐ a. Des O'Connor
   ☐ b. Michael Parkinson
   ☐ c. Jerry Springer

10. **Which swanky London hotel was stormed by a mob of disgruntled Eastenders in September 1941?**

    ☐ a. The Savoy
    ☐ b. Grosvenor House
    ☐ c. The Ritz

11. **Which author did not lose a London house to German bombing?**

    ☐ a. Virginia Woolf
    ☐ b. Graham Greene
    ☐ c. George Orwell

12. **What London bridge was built and opened during the Second World War?**

    ☐ a. London
    ☐ b. Waterloo
    ☐ c. Southwark

13. **Grosvenor Square, site of the embassy and heart of the American compound in wartime London, picked up which temporary nickname?**

    ☐ a. Eisenhower Platz
    ☐ b. Roosevelt Row
    ☐ c. Patton Alley

14. **Which of the following types of World War II gas mask does the Museum of London have on display?**

    ☐ a. A Mickey Mouse gas mask for a child
    ☐ b. An oversize gas mask for a horse
    ☐ c. A miniature gas mask produced to use in a puppet film

15. **What was the going rate for an ex-U.S. services handgun in 1945?**

    ☐ a. £5
    ☐ b. £10
    ☐ c. £25

16. **Which London-born playwright was knocked unconscious by an angry soldier during the VE day celebrations?**

☐ a. Arnold Wesker
☐ b. Harold Pinter
☐ c. John Osborne

17. **London Transport's Chiswick works stopped building buses for the duration, instead producing what?**

☐ a. Aircraft
☐ b. Artillery
☐ c. Tanks

18. **The residents of Swiss Cottage, like many Londoners, spent many nights of the Blitz below ground in their local tube station. What did they do to pass the time?**

☐ a. Wrote and put on plays
☐ b. Played cards
☐ c. Created their own newspaper

19. **What did one BBC newsreader do when Broadcasting House sustained a direct hit on 15 October 1940?**

☐ a. He carried on reading the news, as if nothing had happened
☐ b. He sang the national anthem
☐ c. He called upon the British Government to surrender to Germany

20. When Glen Miller and his band arrived in London on 29 June 1944, they were forced to spend their first night in the capital in which tube station?

☐ a. Sloane Square
☐ b. Leicester Square
☐ c. Piccadilly

N HALL

CHARLES
DICKENS

GRAY'S
INN RD

KINGS
ROAD

DOUGHTY ST

SOME DISTINCTIVE WRITERS

BURY

EDWIN LEAR · GEO. ELIOT · CONAN DOYL
THE LAMBS · THACKERAY · Wᵐ BLAK

. HOSPITAL

ND ST.

some REBELS & MART

PRUDENTIAL JOHN BALL RICHARD II · MA

Literary London

1. **Which famous French writer's stay in London is commemorated by a plaque in Maiden Lane?**

   ☐ a. Arthur Rimbaud
   ☐ b. Voltaire
   ☐ c. Jean-Jacques Rousseau

2. **Which fictional character gives his name to a pub in Northumberland Street, WC2?**

   ☐ a. Mr. Pickwick
   ☐ b. Robinson Crusoe
   ☐ c. Sherlock Holmes

3. **Why is it slightly surprising that there is a statue of the Scottish poet Robbie Burns in Victoria Embankment Gardens?**

   ☐ a. There are no other statues in the Gardens
   ☐ b. He never visited London
   ☐ c. He wrote a poem expressing his hatred of statues

4. **Which eponymous hero of a well-known novel moved from 'Old Jewry to Fetter Lane, and from thence to Wapping'?**

   ☐ a. Lemuel Gulliver
   ☐ b. David Copperfield
   ☐ c. Tristram Shandy

5. **Which Romantic poet was once found sleepwalking in Leicester Square?**

   ☐ a. Byron
   ☐ b. Shelley
   ☐ c. Keats

6. **Which well-known children's author worked for many years as Secretary to the Bank of England in Threadneedle Street?**

    ☐ a.   A. A. Milne
    ☐ b.   Arthur Ransome
    ☐ c.   Kenneth Grahame

7. **Which writer lived for ten years in a house in Gough Square off Fleet Street which is now a museum dedicated to his life and work?**

    ☐ a.   Charles Dickens
    ☐ b.   Dr. Johnson
    ☐ c.   Thomas Carlyle

8. **In Inner Temple Gardens there is a statue of a boy holding a book with the inscription, 'Lawyers, I suppose, were children once'. Who wrote these words?**

    ☐ a.   Oscar Wilde
    ☐ b.   Charles Lamb
    ☐ c.   Jerome K. Jerome

9. **In Dickens's *Oliver Twist* where is Mr. Brownlow standing when he is robbed of his handkerchief by the Artful Dodger?**

    ☐ a.   At a bookstall near Clerkenwell Green
    ☐ b.   Outside a jeweller's in Hatton Garden
    ☐ c.   By a flower shop in Covent Garden

10. **From which London club did Phileas Fogg set off on his journey around the world in eighty days in the novel by Jules Verne?**

  ☐ a. The Beefsteak Club
  ☐ b. The Reform Club
  ☐ c. The Traveller's Club

11. **The wife of which European dramatist ran a notorious nightclub and cabaret in Heddon Street off Regent Street just before the First World War?**

  ☐ a. Henrik Ibsen
  ☐ b. Anton Chekhov
  ☐ c. August Strindberg

12. **Which London pub, mentioned more than a dozen times in Charles Dickens's *The Pickwick Papers*, is the headquarters of the City Pickwick Club?**

  ☐ a. The George and Vulture
  ☐ b. Ye Olde Cheshire Cheese
  ☐ c. The Magpie

13. **Which children's author donated the royalties from his most famous work to the Hospital for Sick Children in Great Ormond Street?**

  ☐ a. Arthur Ransome
  ☐ b. Kenneth Grahame
  ☐ c. J. M. Barrie

14. **Which famous literary pair supposedly first met at St. Bartholomew's Hospital?**

    ☐ a. Dr. Johnson and James Boswell
    ☐ b. Dr. Watson and Sherlock Holmes
    ☐ c. Dr. Jekyll and Mr. Hyde

15. **Which eighteenth-century novelist died in poverty at 41 Old Bond Street?**

    ☐ a. Lawrence Sterne
    ☐ b. Henry Fielding
    ☐ c. Tobias Smollett

16. **Why did thugs beat up the poet John Dryden in Rose Alley, Covent Garden, in December 1679?**

    ☐ a. They were hired to do so by the Earl of
          Rochester who believed that Dryden had
          criticised him in a poem
    ☐ b. They were hired by the Protestant Duke of
          Albemarle who was outraged by Dryden's
          conversion to Catholicism
    ☐ c. They were hired by the Earl of Wharton who
          believed that Dryden had seduced his daughter

17. **Which writer lived at 10 Henrietta Street, Covent Garden, when she visited London?**

    ☐ a. Charlotte Brontë
    ☐ b. George Eliot
    ☐ c. Jane Austen

18. **Why was the crime writer Raymond Chandler thrown out of the Connaught Hotel in Carlos Place when he was staying there in 1955?**

☐ a. It was discovered he had a woman in his room
☐ b. The manager hated his novels
☐ c. He became drunk and insulted other guests in the dining room

19. **What did Dr. Samuel Johnson investigate in Cock Lane in 1762?**

☐ a. A murder
☐ b. A ghost
☐ c. A disappearance

20. **Which fictional character lived at the fictional address of 27A Wimpole Street?**

☐ a. Henry Higgins in George Bernard Shaw's play *Pygmalion*
☐ b. Dracula in Bram Stoker's novel *Dracula*
☐ c. Mr. Pooter in George and Weedon Grossmith's novel *The Diary of a Nobody*

1. **What unusual room can be found at the heart of Leighton House in Holland Park Road?**

   ☐ a. An Arab hall inspired by a twelfth-century Moorish palace in Sicily
   ☐ b. A Japanese temple based on a similar building in Kyoto
   ☐ c. A Minoan courtyard inspired by the Palace of Minos unearthed at Knossos in Crete

2. **What was the original name for Wigmore Hall, the famous venue for classical music recitals on Wigmore Street?**

   ☐ a. Bechstein Hall
   ☐ b. Portman Hall
   ☐ c. Grosvenor Hall

3. **What makes the George in Borough High Street, Southwark, a particularly noteworthy pub?**

   ☐ a. It is the pub in which Chaucer's pilgrims gathered in *The Canterbury Tales*
   ☐ b. It is the only surviving galleried inn in London
   ☐ c. It is the only London pub with its own brewery on the premises

4. **What did an MP named Edward Watkin begin to build at Wembley in the 1890s?**

   ☐ a. A tower that was planned to be 150 feet taller than the Eiffel Tower
   ☐ b. A pyramid ninety feet high to house his own tomb
   ☐ c. A giant statue of Queen Victoria

5. **Which famous building was destroyed by fire on the night of 30 November 1936?**

   ☐ a. The Houses of Parliament
   ☐ b. The Crystal Palace
   ☐ c. The Royal Opera House

6. **What is unusual about the houses at 23 and 24 Leinster Gardens?**

   ☐ a. They have only front façades
   ☐ b. They are built to resemble a medieval castle
   ☐ c. They are four storeys in height but only one room in width

7. **Which London building is decorated with a sculpture by Eric Gill of the characters Prospero and Ariel from Shakespeare's play *The Tempest*?**

   ☐ a. The Royal Courts of Justice
   ☐ b. Broadcasting House
   ☐ c. The Savoy Hotel

8. **Which London sporting arena is sometimes known as 'Billy Williams' Cabbage Patch'?**

   ☐ a. Wembley Stadium
   ☐ b. Lord's Cricket Ground
   ☐ c. Twickenham Rugby Union Ground

9. **Where in London can Sir Paul Pindar's house be found?**

   ☐ a. Holborn
   ☐ b. South Kensington
   ☐ c. Bishopsgate

10. **What creature sits on top of the weathervane on the Royal Exchange?**

    ☐ a. An eagle
    ☐ b. A bull
    ☐ c. A grasshopper

11. **What was founded in 1123 by Rahere, jester to Henry I?**

    ☐ a. London's oldest church
    ☐ b. London's oldest hospital
    ☐ c. London's oldest public house

12. **The Ministry of Sound is a famous nightclub in Gaunt Street. What was the building before it became a club?**

    ☐ a. A bus garage
    ☐ b. A banana warehouse
    ☐ c. A supermarket

13. **Which building at the Royal Botanic Gardens in Kew was constructed as a surprise for Princess Augusta in 1762?**

    ☐ a. The Pagoda
    ☐ b. The Palm House
    ☐ c. The Temperate House

14. **Which London hotel once included part of Yugoslavia?**

    ☐ a. Claridge's
    ☐ b. The Savoy
    ☐ c. The Ritz

15. **What motto is inscribed above the main entrance of the Old Bailey?**

    ☐ a. 'Nation Shall Speak Peace Unto Nation'
    ☐ b. 'Omnia Omnibus Ubique'
    ☐ c. 'Defend the children of the poor and punish the wrongdoer'

16. **What nickname has been given to the Swiss Re building in St. Mary Axe?**

    ☐ a. The Ark
    ☐ b. The Gherkin
    ☐ c. The Glass Egg

17. **What is the name of the large statue which sits on top of the Wellington Arch at the northwest corner of Green Park?**

    ☐ a. 'The Angel of Christian Charity'
    ☐ b. 'Peace Descending on the Quadriga of War'
    ☐ c. 'The Burghers of Calais'

18. **A temple to which Roman god was discovered in 1954 when the foundations of an office block were being dug in the City?**

    ☐ a. Mithras
    ☐ b. Jupiter
    ☐ c. Apollo

19. **What nickname was once given to the National Gallery in Trafalgar Square?**

    ☐ a. The National Sauce Boat
    ☐ b. The National Cruet Stand
    ☐ c. The National Pepperpot

20. Who lived in Kelmscott House, Upper Mall, Hammersmith?

☐ a. William Morris
☐ b. William Gladstone
☐ c. William Kelmscott

Roads & Rivers

LONDON QUIZ

1. **According to one story, how did Knightsbridge get its name?**

   ☐ a. In the early fifteenth century a man named Esmond Knight won the land in a royal tournament and built a bridge there
   ☐ b. In medieval times two knights met in a duel on a bridge over the River Westbourne
   ☐ c. In the twelfth century, it was a place where cattle crossed the river and it was originally 'Neatsbridge' from an old word for cattle

2. **How has Mornington Crescent featured most regularly on BBC Radio over the last few decades?**

   ☐ a. It is the name given to a spoof game featured on the Radio 4 show *I'm Sorry I Haven't a Clue*
   ☐ b. It is the site of the main BBC weather station in London
   ☐ c. It is where one of the reporters who monitor the traffic coming in to London on the Radio 1 Breakfast show stands each morning

3. **The Thames Tunnel was the first underwater tunnel in the world. Where did it run?**

   ☐ a. From Wapping to Rotherhithe
   ☐ b. From Rotherhithe to Limehouse
   ☐ c. From Pimlico to Vauxhall

4. **Why is Coptic Street so called?**

   - [ ] a. It was renamed in the year that the British Museum bought a valuable collection of Coptic manuscripts
   - [ ] b. It was the site of a Coptic church
   - [ ] c. It was home to London's small Coptic community

5. **How many people died in the great Thames flood of January 1928?**

   - [ ] a. No one, but Noel Coward reported that the turn-ups on his trousers 'got frightfully wet'
   - [ ] b. Fourteen people
   - [ ] c. Forty people

6. **How does Piccadilly get its name?**

   - [ ] a. From a slang term for the prostitutes who gathered there in the sixteenth century
   - [ ] b. From Rupert Pickerdell, a landowner at the time of the Civil War
   - [ ] c. From an old word for a kind of starched collar

7. **What unusual item of street furniture can be found in Carting Lane?**

   - [ ] a. A postal box that is green rather than red
   - [ ] b. A gas lamp lit by methane from a sewer beneath
   - [ ] c. A street sign in which the words have been translated into Latin

8. **Which Thames crossing was referred to as the 'Bridge of Sighs' and was the fashionable crossing to leap from in the nineteenth century?**

   ☐ a. Waterloo
   ☐ b. Blackfriars
   ☐ c. Tower

9. **What London street means literally old town or settlement?**

   ☐ a. Old Kent Road
   ☐ b. Aldwych
   ☐ c. Hoxton

10. **What London street was once known as Tyburn Road?**

    ☐ a. Oxford Street
    ☐ b. Edgware Road
    ☐ c. Euston Road

11. **Beside which river did Nelson and Lady Hamilton fish for trout?**

    ☐ a. Wandle
    ☐ b. Thames
    ☐ c. Walbrook

12. **Deptford or the 'deep ford' gets its name from a crossing point of which river?**

    ☐ a. Ravensbourne
    ☐ b. Effra
    ☐ c. Tyburn

13. **Grub Street immortalized by Samuel Johnson in his dictionary as 'originally a street inhabited by writers of small histories, dictionaries, and temporary poems', was renamed what in 1830?**

    ☐ a. Shakespeare Street
    ☐ b. Milton Street
    ☐ c. Pepys Street

14. **Three rivers converge near Vauxhall Bridge. Which of the following does not?**

    ☐ a. Effra
    ☐ b. Thames
    ☐ c. Neckinger

15. **Of which Soho street did John Strype, in his 1720 Survey of London write: 'This street is broad, and the Houses well-built, but of no great Account for its inhabitants which are chiefly French'?**

    ☐ a. Dean Street
    ☐ b. Greek Street
    ☐ c. Old Compton Street

16. **In the 1880s and in the 1950s the Thames was declared biologically dead. How many fish species are there today?**

    ☐ a. Less than 50
    ☐ b. More than 100
    ☐ c. Between 50 and 100

17. **There are many mythological rivers and streams supposedly running under London but which of the following holds no water today?**

    ☐ a. Beverley Brook
    ☐ b. Walbrook
    ☐ c. Houndsditch

18. **The St. James's thoroughfare Pall Mall gets its name from what?**

    ☐ a. The property speculator Paul Mall who first laid the road
    ☐ b. A ball game played with mallets, not unlike croquet
    ☐ c. The Anglo-French term for a boggy wasteland or 'Poor Moor'

19. **A section of which now-sublimated river provides Hyde Park with its Serpentine lake and still passes over Sloane Square tube station in an aqueduct?**

    ☐ a. The Effra
    ☐ b. The Langbourne
    ☐ c. The Westbourne

20. **The valley of which buried river has Seacoal Lane, Newcastle Alley and Turnaround Lane next to it?**

    ☐ a. The Fleet
    ☐ b. The Walbrook
    ☐ c. The Stead

Shops & Shopping

1. **Which once grand department store building now houses the offices of the *Daily Mail* and the *Evening Standard* newspapers?**

   ☐ a. Barkers on Kensington High Street
   ☐ b. Woolworths on Marylebone High Street
   ☐ c. Jones's on the Holloway Road

2. **The legendary 1960s and 1970s clothing label Biba had its final home in which former Kensington High Street department store?**

   ☐ a. Tom and Jerry
   ☐ b. Daisy and Tom
   ☐ c. Derry and Toms

3. **Where in London did Harrods begin?**

   ☐ a. Stepney
   ☐ b. Stoke Newington
   ☐ c. Shoreditch

4. **The novelist Jeanette Winterson owns an organic food store in a once-neglected Georgian building in Spitalfields. What is it called?**

   ☐ a. Verde's
   ☐ b. Sexing the Cherry
   ☐ c. Oranges Are Not the Only Organic Fruit

5. **What did Selfridges on Oxford Street become the first store in the world to sell in 1928?**

   ☐ a. Nylon stockings
   ☐ b. Bakelite radio sets
   ☐ c. Televisions

6. **James Lock & Co. of St. James's, hatters since 1676, invented which classic piece of head gear?**

   ☐ a. The top hat
   ☐ b. The trilby
   ☐ c. The bowler

7. **In *The Hound of the Baskervilles*, before setting off for the wilds of Devon, Sherlock Holmes buys a map from where?**

   ☐ a. W. H. Smith at Charing Cross Railway Station
   ☐ b. Stanfords on Long Acre, Covent Garden
   ☐ c. The Royal Geographical Society, Kensington

8. **How did William Fortnum of Fortnum and Mason first break into the retail business?**

   ☐ a. He sold his horse to buy a stall at Covent Garden market
   ☐ b. He collected and then sold the leftover candles from Queen Anne's royal palace to help fund his grocery business
   ☐ c. Having caught Queen Anne in a compromising position with a stable groom, Fortnum blackmailed the Queen into buying him a shop

9. **Which famous emporium first opened for business as a linen shop on the corner of Sloane Street in 1813?**

   ☐ a. John Lewis
   ☐ b. Harvey Nichols
   ☐ c. Marks and Spencer

10. **From which bookshop was a teenage Noel Coward caught shoplifting?**

☐ a. Maggs Brothers, Berkeley Square
☐ b. Marks and Co., at 84 Charing Cross Road
☐ c. Hatchard's, Piccadilly

11. **What London store provided the model for Grace Brothers in the 1970s BBC sitcom *Are You Being Served*?**

☐ a. Simpson's, Piccadilly
☐ b. Hung on You, King's Road
☐ c. Peter Jones, Sloane Square

12. **Prince Charles bestowed his first royal warrant on which Jermyn Street gentleman's outfitters?**

☐ a. Harvie and Hudson
☐ b. Turnbull and Asser
☐ c. Dunn and Co.

13. **In the 1930s Christina Foyle, the famously eccentric owner of Foyles bookshop on Charing Cross cabled to Adolf Hilter to ask him what?**

☐ a. To sell her the books the Nazis were planning to burn
☐ b. To come over and sign copies of his memoir *Mein Kampf*
☐ c. To take part in one of the famed Foyles literary lunches with Oswald Mosley and Unity Mitford

14. **The entrepreneur and television personality Sir Alan Sugar cut his teeth on which London street market?**

    ☐ a. Portobello Road
    ☐ b. Bermondsey
    ☐ c. Petticoat Lane

15. **Camden Passage antique market Is held every Wednesday and Saturday in which London district?**

    ☐ a. Islington
    ☐ b. Camden
    ☐ c. Notting Hill

16. **The clothing retailer John Stephen, credited with birthing the Mod style that would characterize Swinging London in the 1960s, was dubbed 'the King of' what?**

    ☐ a. Carnaby St.
    ☐ b. The King's Road
    ☐ c. Portobello Road

17. **What was the name of Mary Quant's first boutique on the King's Road?**

    ☐ a. Bizarre
    ☐ b. Bazaar
    ☐ c. Chelsea Girl

18. Vivienne Westwood and Malcolm McClaren's shop SEX (later Seditionarie) at 430 King's Road originated the punk fashion, selling bondage trousers and T-shirts emblazoned with outrageous images and slogans to a whole generation of spiky-haired kids in the mid-1970s. Who, however, were their next-door neighbours at number 428?

    ☐ a. The Chelsea Conservative Club
    ☐ b. The British Legion Club
    ☐ c. The Chelsea Arts Club

19. Where in London is The Old Curiosity Shop?

    ☐ a. 13 Portsmouth Street, Holborn
    ☐ b. 22 Bow Lane, Cheapside
    ☐ c. 2 Flask Walk, Hampstead

20. In 1907, how did William Whiteley, founder of the famous Whiteleys department store in Bayswater, die?

    ☐ a. He tripped and fell from a window on the third floor of his store
    ☐ b. He was shot dead in his office by a man claiming to be his illegitimate son
    ☐ c. He contracted fatal food poisoning after eating shellfish in the restaurant of his store

1. **Which of the following statements is true of the London Oratory in Brompton Road?**

    - ☐ a. The Sherlock Holmes Society of London meets in the Lady Chapel
    - ☐ b. One of the stained glass windows is dedicated to the Royal Society for the Protection of Birds
    - ☐ c. The KGB once used a recess behind a column near its altar as a place to leave messages for its agents

2. **Whose decapitated body lies buried before the altar of the church of St. Margaret's, Westminster?**

    - ☐ a. Anne Boleyn's
    - ☐ b. The Duke of Monmouth's
    - ☐ c. Sir Walter Raleigh's

3. **Which London church allegedly inspired a baker to create the first tiered wedding cake?**

    - ☐ a. St. Bride's
    - ☐ b. St. Dunstan in the West
    - ☐ c. St. Clement Danes

4. **Which famous sailor is buried in the churchyard at St. Mary's, Lambeth?**

    - ☐ a. Captain Cook
    - ☐ b. Captain Bligh
    - ☐ c. Captain Scott

5. **Which seventh-century Saxon abbot has three London churches dedicated to him?**

    - ☐ a. St. Dunstan
    - ☐ b. St. Botolph
    - ☐ c. St. Magnus

6. **Which London church was described as 'the handsomest barn in England' by its architect?**

   ☐ a. St. Anne's, Soho
   ☐ b. St. Margaret Lothbury
   ☐ c. St. Paul's, Covent Garden

7. **Which organisation was founded by the rector of St. Stephen Walbrook in 1953?**

   ☐ a. Amnesty International
   ☐ b. Samaritans
   ☐ c. Oxfam

8. **To whose memory is All Souls Chapel in St. Paul's Cathedral dedicated?**

   ☐ a. St. Thomas Becket
   ☐ b. Queen Victoria
   ☐ c. Lord Kitchener of Khartoum

9. **Which is the only church in London designed by the Regency architect John Nash?**

   ☐ a. All Saints, Margaret Street
   ☐ b. All Souls, Langham Place
   ☐ c. St. Martin-in-the-Fields, Trafalgar Square

10. **From what does the word 'Royal' derive in the name of the church of St. Michael Paternoster Royal in College Hill?**

   ☐ a. The royal chapel that once adjoined it
   ☐ b. A fourteenth-century merchant named Nicholas Royle
   ☐ c. The town of La Réole in southern France

11. **Which infamous American has a memorial in the crypt of St. Mary's, Battersea?**

    ☐ a. Benedict Arnold
    ☐ b. John Wilkes Booth
    ☐ c. Bruno Hauptmann

12. **Which famous Victorian politician was christened in St. Andrew's, Holborn, in 1817?**

    ☐ a. William Gladstone
    ☐ b. Benjamin Disraeli
    ☐ c. Sir Robert Peel

13. **Which London church has a design based on that of the Erechtheion on the Acropolis in Athens?**

    ☐ a. St. Pancras, Euston Road
    ☐ b. St. George in the East, Wapping
    ☐ c. St. James, Piccadilly

14. **Which London church is associated with John Newton, the eighteenth-century anti-slavery campaigner and author of the hymn 'Amazing Grace'?**

    ☐ a. St. Benet Paul's Wharf
    ☐ b. St. Mary Woolnoth
    ☐ c. St. Magnus the Martyr

15. **In the monument to John Stow in the church of St. Andrew Undershaft what does the sixteenth-century historian of London hold in his right hand?**

    ☐ a. A quill pen
    ☐ b. A Bible
    ☐ c. A cross

16. **Which sport, according to legend, was invented by a rector of St. Clement Danes in the Strand?**

    ☐ a.   Lawn tennis
    ☐ b.   Rugby
    ☐ c.   Netball

17. **What is the nickname often given to the church of St. John's, Smith Square?**

    ☐ a.   Queen Elizabeth's fancy
    ☐ b.   Queen Mary's folly
    ☐ c.   Queen Anne's footstool

18. **In his diary entry for 18 August 1667, Samuel Pepys records that he attended a service at the church of St. Dunstan-in-the-West in Fleet Street. What does he admit to doing during the time he was there?**

    ☐ a.   Eating a dozen oranges
    ☐ b.   Making a pass at a young woman in the congregation
    ☐ c.   Sketching a portrait of the preacher

19. **What anniversary did the church of St. Peter upon Cornhill celebrate in 1979?**

    ☐ a.   1000th
    ☐ b.   1500th
    ☐ c.   1800th

20. **What name did Charles Dickens give to the church of St. Olave's, Hart Street?**

    ☐ a.   St. Ghastly Grim
    ☐ b.   St. Grisly Ghoul
    ☐ c.   St. Grossly Gruesome

London Transport

1. **What departed from outside the now-vanished Yorkshire Stingo tavern in Paddington on 4 July 1829?**

   ☐ a. George Shillibeer's first London omnibus
   ☐ b. George Train's first horse-drawn tram
   ☐ c. Goldsworthy Gurney's first steam-powered coach

2. **The Baker Street and Waterloo Underground Railway opened in 1906. Who shortened its name to Bakerloo?**

   ☐ a. The playwright and wit George Bernard Shaw
   ☐ b. Quex, a writer for the *Evening News*
   ☐ c. Owen Seaman, the editor of the humorous magazine *Punch*

3. **The iconic London bus, the custom-built, open-platform, double-decker Routemaster, was almost called what?**

   ☐ a. The Londoner
   ☐ b. The Roadmaster
   ☐ c. The Master Route

4. **Before numbers were introduced in 1906 how did passengers know which route a London bus served?**

   ☐ a. Hawkers with megaphones were required to walk in front of the buses announcing their destinations
   ☐ b. Smartly-dressed conductors greeted each passenger in turn and asked them where they wanted to go
   ☐ c. The buses were colour-coded

5. **Harry Beck created the diagrammatical London tube map back in 1931. His design, though amended, persists to this day, but at which London station is a copy of his original map on display?**

   ☐ a. Finsbury Park
   ☐ b. Mornington Crescent
   ☐ c. Finchley Central

6. **Which London underground station was the first to have an escalator?**

   ☐ a. Earl's Court
   ☐ b. Aldwych
   ☐ c. Hampstead

7. **By what nickname is the Waterloo and City tube line known?**

   ☐ a. The Shoot
   ☐ b. The Drain
   ☐ c. The Hole

8. **Where did the last London tram run to on 6 July 1952?**

   ☐ a. Woolwich
   ☐ b. New Cross
   ☐ c. Elephant and Castle

9. **Which mythical creatures adorn various parts of St. Pancras station?**

   ☐ a. Griffins
   ☐ b. Wyverns
   ☐ c. Unicorns

10. **There are over forty 'ghost stations' on London's underground network, but what makes North End or Bull and Bush Station between Hampstead and Golders Green especially unusual?**

☐ a. It never opened
☐ b. It was built for the sole use of Frank Pick, the first chief executive of London Transport
☐ c. It was closed after its ceiling caved in to reveal the remains of a plague pit

11. **From 1854 until 1941, the Necropolis Railway carried the capital's dead from Waterloo to which cemetery?**

☐ a. Kensal Green
☐ b. West Norwood
☐ c. Brookwood

12. **The concourse of which London underground station was inspired by Pushkinskaya Station on the Moscow Metro?**

☐ a. Sudbury Town
☐ b. Piccadilly Circus
☐ c. Gants Hill

13. **Mosaics by which British pop artist grace the walls of Tottenham Court Road Underground station?**

☐ a. Richard Hamilton
☐ b. Eduardo Paolozzi
☐ c. Peter Blake

14. Following a petition from Arsenal Football Club, Gillespie Road underground station in Highbury was re-named Arsenal (Highbury Hill) in 1932. For five months in 1939 which other London sporting locale had its own dedicated tube stop?

- ☐ a. Lord's Cricket Ground, Marylebone
- ☐ b. Craven Cottage, Fulham
- ☐ c. White Hart Lane, Tottenham

15. At which London station did Queen Victoria arrive on her first train journey in 1842?

- ☐ a. Victoria
- ☐ b. Baker Street
- ☐ c. Paddington

16. All licensed taxi drivers in the capital need to pass a special test before they can drive one of London's iconic black cabs. What is the test called?

- ☐ a. The Knack
- ☐ b. The Knowledge
- ☐ c. The Genius

17. In 2003, a congestion charge was first introduced for most motorized road users in central London during the day. Which of the following vehicles were not granted exemption from the charge?

- ☐ a. Electronic vehicles
- ☐ b. Motor scooters and motorbikes
- ☐ c. Cars driven by diplomats and consular officials in foreign embassies

18. **In 1956 London Transport, facing a severe labour shortage in a period of almost full employment, began to directly recruit staff from which Caribbean island?**

    ☐ a. Jamaica
    ☐ b. Barbados
    ☐ c. Trinidad

19. **What is the name of the two statues by Jacob Epstein on London Transport's former headquarters at 55 Broadway that were branded obscene and even tarred and feathered when the building first opened in 1929?**

    ☐ a. 'Night and Day'
    ☐ b. 'The Lion and the Unicorn'
    ☐ c. 'Gog and Magog'

20. **What was finally banned on London buses in 1991?**

    ☐ a. Busking
    ☐ b. Drinking alcohol
    ☐ c. Smoking

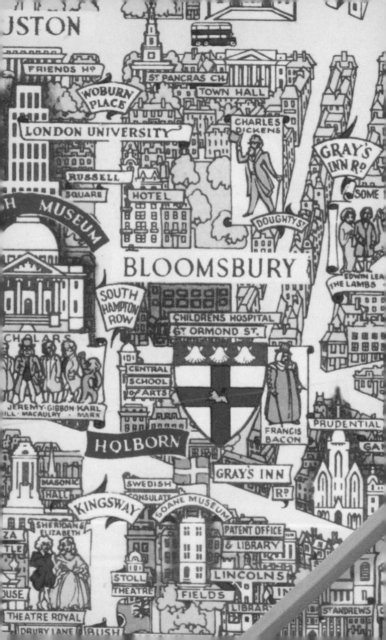

1. **In around 1170, William the Conqueror invited a small group of Jews from Rouen to settle in London. Off which medieval thoroughfare did they make their home?**

    ☐ a. Cheapside
    ☐ b. Watling Street
    ☐ c. Walbrook

2. **In 1189, many Jews were massacred during Richard I's coronation at Westminster Abbey. Where did those who escaped the mob find sanctuary?**

    ☐ a. St. Paul's Cathedral
    ☐ b. The Tower of London
    ☐ c. Guildhall

3. **Where in London was the first synagogue following resettlement in 1656 established?**

    ☐ a. Creechurch Lane, Leadenhall
    ☐ b. Sandy's Row, Middlesex Street
    ☐ c. Greatorex Street, Whitechapel

4. **The Bevis Marks Synagogue in Aldgate was completed in 1701 and is the oldest synagogue in Britain still in use. Which English monarch donated an oak beam from a royal warship for its roof?**

    ☐ a. William III
    ☐ b. Queen Anne
    ☐ c. James II

5. **The National Holocaust Memorial Garden is located in an area of Hyde Park known as what?**

   ☐ a. The Bell
   ☐ b. The Dell
   ☐ c. The Knoll

6. **The Jewish entrepreneur Joseph Moses Levy established the first what in 1855?**

   ☐ a. Ticketing system for London buses
   ☐ b. London penny paper
   ☐ c. Milk bar in London

7. **Which of the following statements about the synagogue in Bevis Marks is true?**

   ☐ a. Most of its original congregation were descended from Jews expelled from Russia
   ☐ b. Its first rabbi was a convert from Methodism
   ☐ c. Its builder was a Quaker

8. **A drinking fountain was erected opposite the London Hospital Whitechapel by the Jews of the East End in 1911 as a memorial to whom?**

   ☐ a. Edward VII
   ☐ b. William S. Gilbert, of Gilbert and Sullivan
   ☐ c. Gustav Mahler

9. The Spitalfields-born Jewish artist Mark Gertler, who committed suicide in 1939, is commemorated with a blue plaque at 32 Elder Street. A replica of which of his paintings is etched into the coal hole on the pavement outside this address?

☐ a. *Supper*
☐ b. *Merry-go-round*
☐ c. *The Fruit-Sorters*

10. C.H.N. Katz was one of the last Jewish businesses to continue trading on Brick Lane. What did Mr. Katz sell?

☐ a. Boxes and crates
☐ b. String and paper bags
☐ c. Cigars and tobacco

11. From which Spitalfields address did the eccentric Cabbalistic scholar David Rodinsky supposedly 'vanish'?

☐ a. 19 Hanbury Street
☐ b. 19 Princelet Street
☐ c. 19 Fashion Street

12. Where did Jewish East Enders defeat Oswald Mosley's 'black shirts' on 4 October 1936?

☐ a. Cable Street
☐ b. Commercial Road
☐ c. Cambridge Heath Road

13. **What part of London is the most Orthodox Jewish area outside of New York and Israel?**

    ☐ a. Golders Green
    ☐ b. Hendon
    ☐ c. Stamford Hill

14. **The London Jewish Cultural Centre is located in whose former Golders Green home?**

    ☐ a. Sigmund Freud
    ☐ b. Anna Pavlova
    ☐ c. Evelyn Waugh

15. **Where in London can you find a statue to Benjamin Disraeli, the first Jewish-born MP to become British Prime Minister?**

    ☐ a. Parliament Square
    ☐ b. Leicester Square
    ☐ c. Trafalgar Square

16. **In the 1830s, which classic London square was initially designed by the Jewish-born architect George Basevi?**

    ☐ a. Belgrave Square
    ☐ b. Berkeley Square
    ☐ c. Brunswick Square

17. **When did Bloom's famed kosher restaurant on Whitechapel High Street close its doors?**

    ☐ a. 1976
    ☐ b. 1986
    ☐ c. 1996

18. **What commemorates the (all too brief) life and work of the Jewish suffragette Minnie Lansbury on the side of the Electric Building, Bow Road?**

   ☐ a. A lamp
   ☐ b. A clock
   ☐ c. A bell

19. **What was the name of the Jewish boxer who knocked out Georgian London?**

   ☐ a. Daniel Mendoza
   ☐ b. Daniel Barenboim
   ☐ c. Daniel Meneka

20. **12 Hanbury Street, Spitalfields, was the birthplace of which popular Jewish wartime entertainer?**

   ☐ a. Vera Lynn
   ☐ b. Bud Flanagan
   ☐ c. Tommy Trinder

London Firsts

1. **What did Joseph Merlin demonstrate for the first time at a masquerade party in Soho in 1760?**

   ☐ a. The kaleidoscope
   ☐ b. Roller skates
   ☐ c. The penny farthing bicycle

2. **What 'first' did John Richard Archer achieve in Battersea in 1913?**

   ☐ a. He was the first Londoner to fly across the Thames in an aeroplane
   ☐ b. He was the first man in Britain to have an organ replaced in a surgical operation
   ☐ c. He became Britain's first black mayor

3. **What invention was first demonstrated in a room above what is now the Bar Italia restaurant in Frith Street, Soho?**

   ☐ a. The espresso coffee machine
   ☐ b. The television
   ☐ c. The vacuum cleaner

4. **What was the first London monument to be damaged in an enemy air attack?**

   ☐ a. Cleopatra's Needle
   ☐ b. The Monument
   ☐ c. Marble Arch

5. **What 'first' opened in Portman Square in 1810?**

   ☐ a. The first department store
   ☐ b. The first theatre to be lit by gaslight
   ☐ c. The first Indian restaurant in London

6. **Who gave his name to Flamsteed House in Greenwich Park?**

   - ☐ a.   The first Poet Laureate
   - ☐ b.   The first Master of the King's Music
   - ☐ c.   The first Astronomer Royal

7. **For which London 'first' was a nineteenth-century colonel named Pierpoint responsible?**

   - ☐ a.   The first escalator
   - ☐ b.   The first traffic island
   - ☐ c.   The first lottery

8. **Where was London's first cab rank?**

   - ☐ a.   In Piccadilly
   - ☐ b.   In The Strand
   - ☐ c.   In Oxford Street

9. **What was the first work of art to occupy the empty 'fourth plinth' in Trafalgar Square?**

   - ☐ a.   Rachel Whiteread's *House*
   - ☐ b.   Tracey Emin's *My Bed*
   - ☐ c.   Mark Wallinger's *Ecce Homo*

10. **Where was London's first ferris wheel erected in 1895?**

   - ☐ a.   Earl's Court
   - ☐ b.   Clapham Common
   - ☐ c.   Green Park

11. **What was first invented in the 1750s by James Ayscough, a maker of optical and scientific instruments, in Ludgate Hill?**

    ☐ a. The magic lantern
    ☐ b. Sunglasses
    ☐ c. 3-D spectacles

12. **What was first recorded and named in Camberwell in August 1748?**

    ☐ a. A species of beetle that was called the Camberwell Stag Beetle
    ☐ b. A species of bird that was called Baird's Camberwell Snipe
    ☐ c. A species of butterfly that was called the Camberwell Beauty

13. **Who was the first prisoner to escape from the Tower of London?**

    ☐ a. Ranulf Flambard, a medieval Bishop of Durham
    ☐ b. Sir John Oldcastle, a leader of the religious reformers known as the Lollards
    ☐ c. Father John Gerard, a Jesuit priest in Elizabethan England

14. **Which 'first' was built in 1868 at the intersection of Great George Street and Bridge Street near Westminster Bridge?**

    ☐ a. The first red postbox
    ☐ b. The first telephone box
    ☐ c. The first set of traffic lights

15. **Which London 'first' took place in a ground-floor room at Brown's Hotel in Dover Street in 1876?**

    ☐ a. The first recording of the human voice
    ☐ b. The first radio message
    ☐ c. The first telephone call

16. **What London 'first' is commemorated by a plaque in St. Michael's Alley off Cornhill?**

    ☐ a. The first insurance company
    ☐ b. The first coffeehouse
    ☐ c. The first American embassy

17. **What was invented in a workshop in Hatton Gardens in the 1880s?**

    ☐ a. The first machine gun
    ☐ b. The first grenade launcher
    ☐ c. The first tank

18. **What unenviable 'first' did Robert Cocking achieve in Vauxhall Gardens?**

    ☐ a. He was the first person in Britain to die in a railway accident
    ☐ b. He was the first person in Britain to die in a ballooning accident
    ☐ c. He was the first person in Britain to die in a parachuting accident

19. **What 'first' did Frederick William Bremer build in Walthamstow in the 1890s?**

    ☐ a. The first car with a petrol-driven internal combustion engine to run on London roads
    ☐ b. The first refrigerator to freeze food successfully
    ☐ c. The first wireless that was able to transmit messages more than a mile

20. **What criminological 'first' in 1905 involved two brothers named Stratton and a robbery in Deptford High Street?**

    ☐ a. First case in which an identikit portrait was issued by the police
    ☐ b. First case in which fingerprints were used to secure a murder conviction
    ☐ c. First case in which the verdict was overturned in the Appeal Court

Lost London

1. **Where did Marble Arch stand between 1827 and 1851?**

   ☐ a.   Outside Buckingham Palace
   ☐ b.   In Hyde Park
   ☐ c.   At Piccadilly Circus

2. **In the eighteenth century, what stood at 60-62, St. Martin's Lane?**

   ☐ a.   The studio of the portrait painter Sir Joshua Reynolds
   ☐ b.   The workshop of the silversmith Paul de Lamerie
   ☐ c.   The business premises of the furniture maker Thomas Chippendale

3. **In which building, now demolished, did the twenty-five-inch tall American Charles Stratton known as General Tom Thumb, make his first appearance in London?**

   ☐ a.   The Pantheon in Oxford Street
   ☐ b.   The Egyptian Hall in Piccadilly
   ☐ c.   Astley's Amphitheatre in Lambeth

4. **Which department store in Holborn, now closed, was known as 'The People's Popular Emporium'?**

   ☐ a.   Swan & Edgar
   ☐ b.   Bon Marché
   ☐ c.   Gamages

5. **For what was the Exeter Exchange, a large building on the north side of the Strand, most famous in the early nineteenth century?**

   ☐ a.   Its swimming pool
   ☐ b.   Its menagerie
   ☐ c.   Its skating rink

6. **Which London jail, the birthplace of Little Dorrit in Charles Dickens's novel of that name, once stood in Borough High Street, Southwark?**

    ☐ a.   The Clink
    ☐ b.   Coldbath Fields
    ☐ c.   The Marshalsea

7. **What was 'The Skylon' which once stood on the South Bank between Waterloo Bridge and Hungerford Bridge?**

    ☐ a.   A sculpture
    ☐ b.   An aeroplane
    ☐ c.   A skyscraper

8. **Which building stood on the site of the present Methodist Central Hall, opposite Westminster Abbey, between 1876 and 1903?**

    ☐ a.   The Royal Menagerie
    ☐ b.   The Royal Aquarium
    ☐ c.   The Royal Exchange

9. **What was The Hippodrome which stood in Notting Hill between 1837 and 1842?**

    ☐ a.   A theatre which specialised in bloody melodramas
    ☐ b.   A racecourse, described by contemporaries as 'more extensive and attractive than Ascot or Epsom'
    ☐ c.   A covered market built by the philanthropist Angela Burdett-Coutts

10. **What reminder of Roman London was unearthed during the construction of an underpass near Blackfriars Bridge in 1962?**

    ☐ a. A mosaic
    ☐ b. A sarcophagus
    ☐ c. A barge

11. **Which London railway terminus once had a seventy-two-foot-high Doric arch at its entrance?**

    ☐ a. Euston
    ☐ b. King's Cross
    ☐ c. Waterloo

12. **What did James Wyld build in the centre of Leicester Square in 1851?**

    ☐ a. A Giant Pagoda
    ☐ b. A Great Globe
    ☐ c. A Grand Glasshouse

13. **Which artist lived at 13 Hercules Buildings, Hercules Road, Lambeth between 1791 and 1800 on a site now occupied by a block of flats named after him?**

    ☐ a. John Constable
    ☐ b. J.M.W. Turner
    ☐ c. William Blake

14. **What was the Temple of Health and Hymen that, in the middle of the eighteenth century, stood in Pall Mall?**

    ☐ a. A brothel
    ☐ b. A place of worship
    ☐ c. A clinic

15. **In the eighteenth and nineteenth centuries, Almack's Assembly Rooms in King Street were the venue for London's most fashionable and socially exclusive balls. Why was the Duke of Wellington once denied admission?**

    ☐ a.   Because he was wearing trousers
    ☐ b.   Because he was smoking a large cigar
    ☐ c.   Because he was Irish

16. **Which famous London building stands on the site where the French chef Alexis Soyer opened a restaurant complex called the 'Gastronomic Symposium of All Nations' in 1851?**

    ☐ a.   Royal Albert Hall
    ☐ b.   Victoria & Albert Museum
    ☐ c.   Natural History Museum

17. **What did the nineteenth-century trader Charles Jamrach sell from his long-vanished store on Ratcliff Highway in the East End?**

    ☐ a.   Drugs such as opium and cannabis
    ☐ b.   Exotic animals such as tigers, rhinos and giraffes
    ☐ c.   Wax models of the famous people of the period

18. **Which building now stands on the site of the old Millbank Prison, demolished in 1890?**

    ☐ a.   Tate Britain
    ☐ b.   Tate Modern
    ☐ c.   National Portrait Gallery

19. **In the early fifteenth century, what did Sir Richard (Dick) Whittington pay to have built by the Thames near what is now Southwark Bridge?**

    ☐ a. A chapel
    ☐ b. A market
    ☐ c. A public lavatory

20. **What was the 'Steelyard' that stood on the site of Cannon Street Station from the fourteenth century to the seventeenth century?**

    ☐ a. The London trading centre of the Hanseatic League
    ☐ b. The London market for metals
    ☐ c. A large distillery for the production of alcoholic spirits

1. **John Wilkes was Lord Mayor in 1774 and a well-known radical MP and politician. What kind of memorial to him can be found in Fetter Lane?**

   ☐ a. The only statue of a man with an umbrella in London
   ☐ b. The only statue of a man with one leg
   ☐ c. The only cross-eyed statue in London

2. **What did Marie Grosholtz open in Baker Street in 1835?**

   ☐ a. A waxworks exhibition
   ☐ b. A millinery business
   ☐ c. A shop for the sale of umbrellas and walking sticks

3. **What do Richard Bright, Thomas Addison and Thomas Hodgkin have in common?**

   ☐ a. They were all members of Dr. Johnson's Literary Club that met at the Turk's Head in Gerrard Street
   ☐ b. They were all doctors at Guy's Hospital who gave their names to diseases
   ☐ c. They were all cricketers who played in the very first match at the new Lord's Cricket Ground in St. John's Wood

4. **Which famous actress is depicted in a statue on the south side of Paddington Green facing the Marylebone flyover?**

   ☐ a. Sarah Siddons
   ☐ b. Ellen Terry
   ☐ c. Edith Evans

5. **Which area of London supposedly takes its name from that of the landlord of a pub in the early seventeenth century?**

☐ a. Parsons Green
☐ b. Pentonville
☐ c. Pimlico

6. **A blue plaque on a house in St. James's Square marks the former home of Ada, Countess of Lovelace. She was the daughter of the poet Lord Byron, but she is also remembered for what kind of pioneering scientific work?**

☐ a. She aided the mathematician Charles Babbage in his investigations into the potential of computing machines
☐ b. She was London's first female dentist and was an early proponent of the use of anaesthesia
☐ c. She was a chemist who worked on the production of synthetic dyes

7. **George Grossmith was co-author of a classic work of London humour, *The Diary of a Nobody*, published in 1892. For what else is he famous?**

☐ a. He was a defending barrister in a number of high profile cases at the Royal Courts of Justice
☐ b. He took major roles in the original productions of Gilbert and Sullivan operettas at the Savoy Theatre
☐ c. He was a brewer who owned a well-known brewery in Whitechapel

8. **Which famous nineteenth-century American writer spent several years at school in Stoke Newington?**

   ☐ a. Herman Melville
   ☐ b. Mark Twain
   ☐ c. Edgar Allan Poe

9. **What was the day job of Frederick John Horniman who created the Horniman Museum in Forest Hill and presented it to the London County Council in 1901?**

   ☐ a. He was a jeweller
   ☐ b. He was a tea merchant
   ☐ c. He was a fur trader

10. **For what achievement is Lilian Baylis best remembered?**

   ☐ a. She ran the Old Vic theatre in the first half of the twentieth century
   ☐ b. She was the first woman to enter the House of Commons
   ☐ c. She was the architect of Broadcasting House in Portland Place

11. **Which music hall performer was born in Agar Town, a slum area now covered by St. Pancras Station, and was the first to give a Royal Command Performance?**

   ☐ a. Marie Lloyd
   ☐ b. Albert Chevalier
   ☐ c. Dan Leno

12. **Who was the 'Stepney Amazon'?**

   ☐ a. A nineteenth-century circus performer
   ☐ b. A cross-dressing woman who served in the British army
   ☐ c. The female boss of an East End criminal gang

13. **The birth of Susanna Annesley in a house in Spital Yard, Bishopsgate, is recorded in a plaque on the site. As what is she most famous?**

   ☐ a. The mother of John Wesley
   ☐ b. The wife of John Milton
   ☐ c. The mother-in-law of David Garrick

14. **Where was Sir Isaac Newton living just before he moved to the site in Jermyn Street which is now marked by a blue plaque?**

   ☐ a. In the Royal Mint—he was its Master
   ☐ b. In the Bank of England—he was its Chief Cashier
   ☐ c. In Gresham College, Bishopsgate—he was its Professor of Astronomy

15. **Who opened an ophthalmic practice in Upper Wimpole Street in 1891?**

   ☐ a. The cricketer, Dr. W. G. Grace
   ☐ b. The murderer, Dr. Hawley Harvey Crippen
   ☐ c. The writer, Dr. Arthur Conan Doyle

16. **Which famous Londoner was born in a house in Salisbury Court?**

   ☐ a. Dr. Johnson
   ☐ b. Charles Dickens
   ☐ c. Samuel Pepys

17. **What do the writers Raymond Chandler, P. G. Wodehouse and C. S. Forester all have in common?**

☐ a. They all worked for the Bank of England in Threadneedle Street

☐ b. They all went to school at Dulwich College

☐ c. They all contributed to revue shows staged at the Whitehall Theatre in the 1920s

18. **What cocktail takes its name from a Billingsgate shellfish dealer who opened an oyster bar in Poultry in 1823?**

☐ a. Harvey Wallbanger

☐ b. Pimm's No. 1

☐ c. Tom Collins

19. **What was unusual about the eighteenth-century writer Gustavus Vassa who lived in Riding House Street?**

☐ a. He was born deaf and dumb

☐ b. He was a slave in the West Indies for ten years

☐ c. He was revealed to be a woman after his death

20. **Samuel Gompers was born in Tenter Street, Spitalfields, in 1850 but left London as a teenager. Which of the following statements about him is true?**

☐ a. There was once a U.S. Navy vessel named after him

☐ b. His birthday is a public holiday in Melbourne

☐ c. There is a town in Canada named after him

1. **What was unusual about the burial of the poet and playwright Ben Jonson in Westminster Abbey in 1637?**

   ☐ a. He was buried standing upright
   ☐ b. He was buried at the stroke of midnight on Christmas Eve
   ☐ c. He was buried more than three months after he had died

2. **In Tooley Street there is a plaque that records the death in 1861 of James Braidwood. Who was he and how did he die?**

   ☐ a. The head of the Thames River Police and he died after being pulled from the river
   ☐ b. The first director of what became the London Fire Brigade and he died in the Great Tooley Street Fire
   ☐ c. Chief Cashier of the Bank of England and he was attacked by a garrotter in the street

3. **After Alfred Linnell died in 1887, thousands of men and women marched behind his coffin from the centre of the city to Bow Cemetery. Why did so many people turn out to honour him?**

   ☐ a. He was killed by the police in the Bloody Sunday demonstrations of that year
   ☐ b. He was a champion jockey and one of the most popular sporting celebrities of Victorian London
   ☐ c. He was a popular hero who had given his life to save three children from a runaway horse

4. **Which London cemetery is divided into a western half and an eastern half by Swains Lane?**

   ☐ a. Kensal Green
   ☐ b. Brompton
   ☐ c. Highgate

5. **What unusual kind of burial ground can be found tucked away in a corner of Kensington Gardens?**

   ☐ a. A dogs' cemetery
   ☐ b. A dolls' cemetery
   ☐ c. A cemetery for suicides

6. **What happened to Georgi Markov on 7 September 1978 to cause his death as he stood at a bus stop at the southern end of Waterloo Bridge?**

   ☐ a. He was stabbed in the thigh with a poisoned umbrella
   ☐ b. He was struck on the head by a stone thrown from the top deck of a passing bus
   ☐ c. He was shot by a marksman in the office building opposite

7. **Thomas Parr is buried in Poets' Corner in Westminster Abbey but he was not a poet. For what is he famous?**

   ☐ a. He helped Charles II to escape from England after the Battle of Worcester in 1651
   ☐ b. He was the father of Catherine Parr, the last of Henry VIII's wives
   ☐ c. He is alleged to have lived to the age of 152

8. **What was unusual about the death in 1864 of a City banker called Thomas Briggs whose body was found on railway tracks between Bow and Hackney Wick?**

    ☐ a. He had fallen from a hot air balloon that had passed overhead
    ☐ b. He was the victim of the first murder on a London train
    ☐ c. He had died from a tropical disease of which he was the first recorded British victim

9. **What is unusual about the memorial in Kensal Green Cemetery to the nineteenth-century circus performer Andrew Ducrow?**

    ☐ a. It is decorated with stone sphinxes
    ☐ b. There is a marble elephant on the top of it
    ☐ c. The inscription on it is written in Sanskrit

10. **What happened in 1747 when the Jacobite Lord Lovat went to his execution on Tower Hill?**

    ☐ a. A grandstand erected for spectators collapsed and twenty people died
    ☐ b. Fellow Jacobites attempted to rescue him and a brawl broke out in which five people were killed
    ☐ c. The King sent a reprieve but the messenger delivering it arrived two minutes after Lovat's head had been struck from his body

11. **The American magician William Robinson, who performed under the name of Chung Ling Soo, died the day after performing at the Wood Green Empire music hall in 1918. What was the cause of his death?**

    ☐ a. He was accidentally struck on the head by a member of the audience he had hypnotised
    ☐ b. He was skewered by two knives thrown at him by a drunken assistant
    ☐ c. He was shot when a rigged gun involved in one of his tricks failed to work properly and fired a real bullet at him

12. **What was the so-called 'Fatal Vespers' that occurred in Blackfriars on 5 November 1623?**

    ☐ a. An accident in the French ambassador's house that killed ninety-five Catholics
    ☐ b. A sword fight between Catholics and Protestants in which several people were killed
    ☐ c. A fire in the Blackfriars Theatre which resulted in the deaths of two actors

13. **Who was Jimmy Garlick?**

    ☐ a. A twentieth-century East End gangster
    ☐ b. A Victorian murderer
    ☐ c. A medieval mummy

14. **What caused the death of eight people in the Tottenham Court Road area on 17 October 1814?**

    ☐ a. The Great London Beer Flood
    ☐ b. The Great London Earthquake
    ☐ c. The Great London Fireworks Explosion

15. Who was the last person to be executed in the Tower of London?

- ☐ a. Henry Laurens, an American spy during the Revolutionary War
- ☐ b. Carl Lody, a German spy during the First World War
- ☐ c. Josef Jakobs, a German spy during the Second World War

16. How did seventeen people die in Princelet Street on 18 January 1888?

- ☐ a. They were crushed to death during a performance at the Hebrew Dramatic Club when a false fire alarm caused a stampede for the exits
- ☐ b. They were buried beneath a wall which collapsed at the Jewish Soup Kitchen
- ☐ c. They were drowned when underground water pipes burst

17. In the churchyard of St. Mary Magdalene in Mortlake there is a mausoleum in the shape of a large Arab tent made of stone. Whose is it?

- ☐ a. An Arab Christian convert named Abu al Khayr who settled in Mortlake in the 1880s and died there in 1896
- ☐ b. Sir Marmaduke Morecombe, one of the earliest Arabic scholars in Britain, who worked on a translation of the Koran, first published in 1783, while living in Mortlake
- ☐ c. Sir Richard Burton, one of the few Europeans to visit Mecca in the nineteenth century, who died in Trieste in 1890 but was taken to Mortlake to be buried by his widow

18. **In 1967, how did the controversial playwright Joe Orton die in his flat in Noel Road, Islington?**

    ☐ a. He choked to death on a fish bone
    ☐ b. He was electrocuted as a result of the flat's poor wiring
    ☐ c. He was battered to death by his lover, Kenneth Halliwell

19. **Where can you find a plaque to a Victorian nursery maid called Alice Ayres who rescued her employer's three children from a fire but died when she tried to leap to safety herself from an upstairs window?**

    ☐ a. Postman's Park
    ☐ b. The crypt of St. Paul's Cathedral
    ☐ c. In one of the wards in St. Thomas's Hospital

20. **Whose 'auto-icon' still sits in a glass-fronted case in University College, London, more than a century and a half after he died?**

    ☐ a. Benjamin Disraeli's
    ☐ b. Jeremy Bentham's
    ☐ c. John Stuart Mill's

LONDON QUIZ

A London Miscellany

1. **Which of the following events have taken place in the Albert Hall in the past twenty-five years?**

   ☐ a. The first Sumo wrestling Grand Basho or major tournament ever to be held outside Japan

   ☐ b. The world championship for German 'oompah' bands

   ☐ c. An indoor marathon for one-legged men and women

2. **What unusual business did Daniel Defoe, the author of *Robinson Crusoe*, run briefly and unsuccessfully in Stoke Newington in the 1690s?**

   ☐ a. Gathering and selling hay to stables

   ☐ b. Running an eel farm

   ☐ c. Breeding civet cats for use in the manufacture of perfume

3. **Who lived at 16 Percy Circus off Pentonville Road during his second visit to London in 1905?**

   ☐ a. Mahatma Gandhi

   ☐ b. V. I. Lenin

   ☐ c. Franklin D. Roosevelt

4. **Which essential aid for visitors to London was the brainchild of Phyllis Pearsall who was born in East Dulwich in 1906?**

   ☐ a. The tube map

   ☐ b. *London A-Z*

   ☐ c. *Time Out* magazine

5. **In what unusual location did fourteen men gather to dine on 23 October 1843?**

   ☐ a. On top of Nelson's Column
   ☐ b. Inside a model dinosaur at Sydenham Hill
   ☐ c. Under the Thames in a tunnel dug by Isambard Kingdom Brunel's father

6. **In March 1952, why did Lord Noel-Buxton walk into the Thames near Westminster Bridge?**

   ☐ a. He was fleeing the enraged husband of his mistress
   ☐ b. He was trying to prove that the river was fordable at that point
   ☐ c. He was measuring the power of the tides at that point

7. **How did the pub called 'The Only Running Footman' in Charles Street get its name?**

   ☐ a. It commemorates Charles Ansell, a servant of the Duke of Northumberland, who was a champion athlete in the early nineteenth century
   ☐ b. A running footman was a servant employed by the wealthy in the eighteenth century to run ahead of their carriages to clear the way and pay any tolls
   ☐ c. It takes the name from a character in a novel by the Victorian novelist Rhoda Broughton

8. **Why did a performance of *La Traviata* at Sadler's Wells theatre have to be abandoned in December 1952?**

   ☐ a. Smog drifting into the theatre was so thick that the audience could scarcely see the performers

   ☐ b. The tenor playing Alfredo Germont died of a heart attack in mid-aria

   ☐ c. Parts of the theatre walls collapsed

9. **Why do cabbies sometimes call the intersection of Kensington Gore and Exhibition Road 'Hot and Cold Corner'?**

   ☐ a. There is a burger bar on one side of it and an ice cream parlour just round the corner

   ☐ b. The Royal Geographical Society building there has two statues on its exterior, one of David Livingstone who explored tropical Africa and one of Ernest Shackleton who explored the icy Antarctic

   ☐ c. The wind often blows icily along Kensington Gore but Exhibition Road is sheltered from it

10. **Who or what is or was Johnston Sans?**

   ☐ a. A well-known music hall performer of the 1890s

   ☐ b. The font used in signage for the London Underground

   ☐ c. A famous department store, now closed, in Kensington High Street

11. **What did Richard Martin, an Irish MP known as 'Humanity Dick', help to found at Old Slaughter's Coffee House in St. Martin's Lane in 1824?**

    ☐ a. The Royal Society for the Prevention of Cruelty to Animals
    ☐ b. The Royal Humane Society
    ☐ c. The Metropolitan Free Drinking Fountain Association

12. **For what type of artwork was Mortlake famous in the seventeenth century?**

    ☐ a. Pottery
    ☐ b. Tapestry
    ☐ c. Miniature painting

13. **What is unusual about the Jamme Masjid mosque in Brick Lane?**

    ☐ a. It was the first mosque to be purpose-built in London
    ☐ b. It is the largest mosque in Western Europe
    ☐ c. It is the only building in the city that has been a place of worship for all three of the world's major monotheistic religions

14. **Where is the last remaining tollgate in London?**

    ☐ a. College Road, Dulwich
    ☐ b. Well Walk, Hampstead
    ☐ c. Strand on the Green, Chiswick

15. **A blue plaque in Denmark Street, WC2, commemorates Augustus Siebe (1788–1872). For what achievement is Siebe best known?**

   ☐ a. He devised a system of classifying clouds
   ☐ b. He invented a type of diving helmet
   ☐ c. He had an enormous music hall hit with a song entitled 'If It Wasn't for the 'Ouses In Between'

16. **In the eighteenth century, which of the following curiosities could be found in Don Saltero's Coffee House in Chelsea?**

   ☐ a. A piece of metal found in the ruins of Troy
   ☐ b. An ingenious flea-trap
   ☐ c. A set of beads made from the bones of St. Anthony of Padua

17. **In eighteenth-century London what were Hawcubites, Mohocks and Tityre-Tus?**

   ☐ a. Political parties
   ☐ b. Upper-class tearaways
   ☐ c. Prostitutes

18. **In Pickering Place off St. James Street, there is a plaque that marks the site of a nineteenth-century embassy to the Court of St. James. Which short-lived nation-state did the embassy represent?**

   ☐ a. Newfoundland
   ☐ b. New South Wales
   ☐ c. Texas

19. **Which area of London gives its name to a Russian word for a railway station?**

    ☐ a. Euston
    ☐ b. Vauxhall
    ☐ c. Victoria

20. **What was blown down from the roof of Westminster Hall during the so-called Great Storm of November 1703?**

    ☐ a. Oliver Cromwell's head
    ☐ b. A statue of Magog, one of the giants which are said to be guardians of the city
    ☐ c. A chimney shaped like one of the towers on the West front of Westminster Abbey

Answers

CRIME AND PUNISHMENT

1. (a) Born in Spitalfields, Sheppard was first arrested for a burglary in Clare Market in 1724. In the course of that year he escaped and was re-arrested four times, becoming a popular hero because of his seemingly magical ability to free himself from bars and chains. After his final capture he was kept in Newgate, weighed down by chains and under constant observation, and eventually taken to the gallows at Tyburn.

2. (b) In the aftermath of the Great Fire, Catholic agents of the Pope and France were blamed for starting it and, for many years, this false accusation was inscribed on the Monument constructed to commemorate the event. Either because he was simple-minded or because he had been tortured, Hubert confessed to starting the fire, despite the fact that he had not even been in London on the day in question.

3. (a) The conspirators hoped to trigger a nationwide uprising, but the group had been infiltrated by government spies and the loft was raided by the Bow Street Runners before the would-be revolutionaries set off for Grosvenor Square. The leader of the gang, Arthur Thistlewood, and four of his followers were hanged outside Newgate Prison three months later.

4. (b) Duell's body had been brought to Surgeons' Hall to be prepared for dissection. When it was being washed, someone noticed that there were signs of life. Duell eventually recovered from the ordeal of execution, he was returned to Newgate Prison and his sentence was changed to transportation. Resurrection men or body snatchers did operate in London, but they usually waited until the bodies had been buried.

5. (c) Execution Dock stood at the side of the Thames between Wapping New Stairs and King Henry's Stairs. It was the place where pirates were hung in the sixteenth and seventeenth centuries and their bodies left in chains until three tides had washed over them. Kidd's execution proved a fiasco. He was so drunk he could barely stand and, as the cart on which he was swaying was moved from the scaffold, the rope around his neck broke and he was thrown to the ground. Still tipsy, and now covered in Thames mud, he was manhandled back on to the cart and eventually dispatched.

6. (a) John George Haigh has come to be known as the 'Acid Bath Murderer'. He was convicted of six murders but may have committed more. He was hanged at Wandsworth Prison in 1949.

7. (b) A bomb was planted outside the wall of the prison in Clerkenwell as part of an attempt to free Richard Burke, a member of the Irish Republican Brotherhood, who was awaiting trial in one of the cells there. Michael Barrett, one of those responsible for the explosion, became the last man to be publicly hanged outside Newgate Prison the following year.

8. (b) As the plaque records, Terriss was the star of the melodramas staged at the Adelphi who 'met his untimely end' outside the theatre when he was stabbed by a deranged fellow-actor. Sir Henry Wilson was killed by IRA gunmen outside his home in Eaton Place; David Blakely was shot by his ex-girlfriend Ruth Ellis as he emerged from the Magdala Tavern in Hampstead.

9. (c) The gunmen were members of the Provisional IRA who were fleeing from the police. After taking Mr. and Mrs.

Matthews hostage, they barricaded themselves into the flat and demanded a plane to take them to Dublin. The siege at Balcombe Street lasted six days but ended peacefully.

10. (c) Jonson killed the actor Gabriel Spenser in a swordfight. He was tried for manslaughter and was eventually released with no worse punishment than branding of his left thumb.

11. (b) Spencer Perceval was shot on 11 May 1812, as he walked through the lobby of the House of Commons, by a deranged businessman called John Bellingham who believed that the government was to blame for the difficulties he had encountered while trading in Russia. One of Bellingham's direct descendants is currently a Conservative MP.

12. (c) The two women were both killed by Jack the Ripper in the early hours of 30 September 1888. Elizabeth Stride was found in a yard off what is now Henriques Street at about 1 am; the body of Catherine Eddowes was found a little later in Mitre Square.

13. (a) 39 Hilldrop Crescent was the family home of Dr. Crippen. In 1910, he fled from it with his mistress Ethel Le Neve, leaving behind the body of Mrs. Crippen in the cellar. He was hanged for the murder of his wife and his waxwork can still be seen in Madame Tussaud's Chamber of Horrors. All the murders attributed to Jack the Ripper took place in the East End; John Reginald Christie killed at least six women in his flat at 10 Rillington Place in Notting Hill.

14. (b) In an article in his brother's political journal *The Examiner*, Hunt had said of the Prince (later George IV) that 'this Adonis in loveliness is a corpulent man of fifty' and that he was a man 'who had just closed half a century without one single claim on the gratitude of his country'. Both Hunts were fined £500 and imprisoned for two years for libelling the Prince. The other two alternative answers were indeed offences at the time, but there is no evidence that Hunt had ever committed them.

15. (a) Greenberry Hill was an alternative name for Primrose Hill which is where Godfrey's body was found in a ditch on 17 October 1678. His murder remains a mystery, although three men called Green, Berry and Hill were indeed named as his killers by an informant and arrested. They were later released.

16. (a) Led by a man named John Lincoln, gangs roamed through the city's streets, attacking and burning houses and workshops belonging to traders from Flanders, Italy, France and the Baltic. Lincoln and several other ringleaders were later hanged.

17. (b) Huge crowds attended public executions at the time. It has been claimed that nearly 40,000 gathered to watch Haggerty and Holloway go to the gallows and people were pressed so closely together that, when the panic started, it was impossible to stop it. Newgate prison stood on the site of what is now the Central Criminal Court, also known as the Old Bailey.

18. (b) As well as being a popular singer, Martha Ray was the mistress of the Earl of Sandwich but she was pursued by another man—a clergyman named James Hackman. In April 1779, the tormented Hackman shot her dead. He was hanged at Tyburn ten days later. Hackman's obsessive love attracted surprising public sympathy and his *crime passionnel* has become one of the best-known London murders of the eighteenth century, fictionalised in novels and the subject of a recent historical investigation.

19. (a) It was assumed that the murderer was Bartlett's French-born wife Adelaide. She was tried and acquitted but many people continued to believe in her guilt. 'Now that it is all over,' one prominent medical man said, 'she should tell us, in the interest of science, how she did it'. She never did.

20. (a) Rose was a cook in the employ of the Bishop of Rochester at his London town house. He attempted to kill the Bishop by putting poison in the soup served at a dinner but succeeded only in murdering sixteen other people. Rose was placed in a cauldron of water and a fire was lit beneath it. He took two hours to die.

LONDON IN THE MOVIES

1. (a) The film is largely autobiographical. In the late 1960s, its writer and director Bruce Robinson was a struggling actor living with another would-be thesp, the bibulous Vivian MacKerrel, in an unheated flat on Albert Street off Parkway. He was so poor that he used to swipe abandoned vegetables off Camden Market.

2. (c) The event is dramatised in the 1951 film *The Magic Box*. This picture starred Robert Donat as Friese-Greene with Sir Laurence Olivier in a cameo role as a policeman startled by this extraordinary sight. Friese-Greene, who also developed an early version of a colour movie, failed to profit from any of his inventions. He died at a conference of the British film industry in London in 1921 and is buried in Highgate Cemetery.

3. (a) The inhabitants are initially delighted as they can claim exemption from the strict restrictions on food, clothing and fuel that then applied to the rest of Britain. Most of the film itself was shot not in Pimlico but directly across the River Thames from it in Lambeth.

4. (c) Stanley Kubrick, who refused to leave his adopted home of Britain, opted to use Beckton when he came to film his Vietnam epic, *Full Metal Jacket* (1987). Palm trees were imported from Spain to help give the impression that his cast were prowling through lush South Asian foliage. In Steven Spielberg's adaption of J. G. Ballard's autobiographical novel *Empire of the Sun*, some scenes depicting the Lunghua Camp outside Shanghai were also shot at Beckton.

5. (b) The picture focuses on a hard-bitten newspaper journalist who is trying to discover why temperatures are soaring. Made in 1961, it provides a glimpse of a now-vanished Fleet Street world. Several scenes were filmed in the old *Daily Express* building on what was then a thoroughfare lined with newspaper offices. The Express's then editor Arthur Christiansen also appeared in the movie as himself.

6. (a) The wolfman, who also rages through Piccadilly and bites the head off a man in Tottenham Court Underground station, finally meets his end in Winchester Walk, Borough, SE1.

7. (c) The restaurant chain was founded by the Hollywood stars Arnold Schwarzenegger, Sylvester Stallone, Bruce Willis and Demi Moore.

8. (c) Based on Nick Hornby's bestselling memoir, the movie was supposedly set in the 1970s and 1980s. Craven Cottage was chosen because it still had terraces. Arsenal's home, Highbury, had become an all-seater stadium by the time the film was shot in 1997.

9. (b) Based on the novel by Gerald Kersh, directed by Jules Dassin in 1950 and starring Richard Widmark as Fabian, the film captures the seedier side of London in luminous black and white.

10. (c) The diabolical Pinhead is brought to life at '66 Lodovico Street'. In reality this was number 187, Dollis Hill Lane, Dollis Hill.

11. (c) Billy, created by Keith Waterhouse and played by Tom Courtenay, never makes it to the capital in this 1963 film. He steps off the train for London just before it is due to depart.

12. (a) Schofield is supposedly journeying about the city in the company of his friend Robinson, an unseen investigator of the capital's history, in Keiller's discursive portrait of the city, made in 1992.

13. (b) Based on a book of the same name by Geoffrey Fletcher, this documentary provides a fascinating portrait of East End pie-and-mash shops, shelters for derelicts and crumbling old music halls.

14. (c) It starred Hugh Jackman, Scarlett Johansson and Ian McShane, but this London-set romantic comedy thriller went straight to DVD in the UK.

15. (a) Justin Chadwick played a Notting Hill drug dealer trying to go straight but lacking the decent footwear needed to take up a job in a local diner.

16. (c) The house belonging to Mrs. Wilberforce, the old lady who thwarts the gang of robbers led by Professor Marcus (Alec Guinness), stands in the station's shadows.

17. (a) Although its front destination board reads: London to the South of France via Dover Paris. A section of the film was shot at London Transport's bus works in Aldenham.

18. (b) The movie's opening murder scene was filmed there.

19. (b) It specialised in travel books and was modelled on the Travel Bookshop at 13-15 Blenheim Crescent, just off Portobello Road.

20. (b) 113 Wardour Street was home to Hammer House. Hammer produced a stream of popular horror pictures between the late 1950s and early 1970s.

MUSICAL LONDON

1. (c) The club was first established beneath a Chinese fan-tan gambling den at 39 Gerrard Street before moving to its current location at 47 Frith Street in 1965. Scott often acted as the club compère and was famed for the droll comic introductions he gave performers. Along with recordings with Tubby Hayes and The Jazz Couriers, Scott's sax can be heard on The Beatles' 'Lady Madonna'.

2. (a) Mozart was brought to London as a child prodigy by his father in 1764. A blue plaque on a house in Ebury Street records that the young genius composed his first symphony there.

3. (b) Despite its capital title track, many of the songs on this album were composed on a yacht moored off the Virgin Islands.

4. (a) Paul Lincoln and Reg Hunter, two Australians involved in the world of wrestling, acquired the lease of the café in the early 1950s. Before that, according to Lincoln, the café 'was owned by three Iranian brothers and they called it the 3 I's. Apparently one of them left and so it ended up as the 2 I's.' Peter Grant, the future manager of Led Zeppelin but then a wrestler, was employed by Lincoln and Hunter during its heyday to man the door.

5. (b) It would be hard to find two musicians more different but Hendrix is said to have been pleased by the coincidence that he was living in a house next door to one in which Handel had composed so much of his music.

6. (b) Holst was music master at the school for many years and also wrote a *Hammersmith Suite* and a *Brook Green Suite*.

7. (c) The name apparently derived from a road sign for 'Kilburn High Road' that Dury often passed on his way to score dope at the El Rio club on the Harrow Road.

8. (b) Meek blasted its proprietor and his landlady, Mrs. Violet Shenton, with a shotgun, before turning the gun on himself on 3 February 1967, the eighth anniversary of the death of his hero Buddy Holly.

9. (a) Outbidding David Bowie, Page acquired the property from the hell-raising actor Richard Harris in 1974. At the time when he was editing *Lucifer Rising*, the occultist filmmaker Kenneth Anger lived in Page's basement.

10. (c) Though Jagger did attend an anti-Vietnam War rally in March 1968 led by Tariq Ali, who is said to have been the inspiration for the song.

11. (c) The Muswell Hill–born Davies had originally composed a song heralding the demise of the so-called Merseybeat groups from Liverpool. However, after The Beatles released 'Penny Lane', he transformed it into a homage to his home city instead.

12. (a) Dylan had come to England that November to appear in a BBC TV play, *The Madhouse on Castle Street*. He used his time in London to check out the capital's folk scene, paying visits to Collets record shop on the Tottenham Court Road and such clubs as Bunjies Coffee House off the Charing Cross Road and the celebrated and still extant Troubadour on Cromwell Road. The Pindar of Wakefield, now The Water Rats, also continues as a venue for live music.

13. (b) Grainger was born in Australia and lived for many years in the USA but he also spent time in London. His residence in King's Road, Chelsea, is now marked by a blue plaque.

14. (c) The Gershwins wrote the song for a film version of P. G. Wodehouse's novel and play *A Damsel in Distress* starring Fred Astaire. George Gershwin never saw the film, however, as he died from a brain tumour in July 1937, some five months before it was completed.

15. (b) It was not a job Berlioz found very congenial. 'It splits your head to hear these hundreds of wretched machines,' he wrote, 'each one more out of tune than the next.'

c) 3 Savile Row. It was from the roof of this building that The Beatles played their final gig.

17. (b) Chopin was already mortally ill with consumption but he agreed to give a performance in aid of Polish refugees. He died in Paris the following year. The house in St. James's Place, SW1, where he stayed on this last visit to London is marked by a blue plaque.

18. (c) Born just down the road at 507 Archway Road, Stewart later maintained the job cured him of his fear of death.

19. (a) Some forty-years after its opening, Brian Epstein cut The Beatles demo disc that assured their audition with George Martin there.

20. (b) In 1938, the *Times* ran a headline that read "While dictators rage and statesmen talk, all Europe dances to 'The Lambeth Walk' ". The song had been popular in Germany, but its composer Noel Gay's noble refusal to sign a document declaring he had no Jewish blood, led to its being banned by the Nazi party. In 1941, an English propaganda newsreel entitled Lambeth Walk-Nazi Style, consequently spliced footage pilfered from Leni Riefenstahl's *Triumph of the Will* to a recording of the song to great comic effect.

THEATRICAL LONDON

1. (c) Garrick was first turned away by the men who ran London's principal theatres at the time and he was forced to make his debut at the Goodman's Fields Theatre in unfashionable

Whitechapel. His performance as Richard III was so remarkable
that word of mouth spread and the theatre was soon packed
every night. The managers of the bigger theatres were eventually
forced to change their minds and invite him onto their stages.

2. (a) Shakespeare had a share in this Bankside theatre and
acted there. Many of his most famous plays, including *Romeo
and Juliet*, *Othello*, *Macbeth* and *King Lear* were first performed at
The Globe.

3. (c) Charing Cross Road. The statue in bronze by Thomas
Brock was paid for with donations from other actors and
unveiled in 1910.

4. (a) Nine years after it opened, W. S. Gilbert fell out with
D'Oyly Carte over a £500 bill for new carpets for the theatre.
Arthur Sullivan took D'Oyly Carte's side in the quarrel. Gilbert
and Sullivan's partnership, while staggering on for two more
operas, never recovered from the dispute.

5. (b) George Bernard Shaw. Shaw served for six years as a
Borough Councillor for St. Pancras, although he had stated
in 1903 that he was convinced that, 'Borough Councils must
be abolished.' In the spring of 1904, he ran as a Progressive
candidate for one of two London County Council seats in South
St. Pancras. He lost and abandoned local politics after that.

6. (c) It was the third production of the new English Stage
Company, under Artistic Director George Devine. In January
1956, Devine had placed an advert in *The Stage* calling for
scripts, and received over 700 submissions, including Osborne's
Look Back in Anger, a play already rejected by Laurence Olivier,

ence Rattigan and Binkie Beaumont. Now credited with being the first 'Kitchen Sink Drama', it opened to empty houses and mostly terrible reviews on 8 May 1956. It took a favourable notice by Kenneth Tynan in *The Observer* to transform its fortunes.

7. (b) There was a train that conveyed the King and his entourage from the entrance hall to the Royal Box. The contraption was said to have broken down the first time it was used, and whether it existed at all remains a matter of some dispute. But the Coliseum, nevertheless, was a hive of gadgetry. It was the first theatre in England to possess a revolving stage and the first in Europe to have an elevator.

8. (a) Collins' Music Hall backed onto New Bunhill Fields, an unconsecrated nonconformist burial ground, which by the time it closed in 1853 was estimated to contain some 15,000 bodies. Collins' burnt down in a fire in 1958 and only the fascia of the original building remains. It is currently home to a branch of Waterstone's bookshops.

9. (c) Barrie bequeathed the royalties to all the Peter Pan novels and plays to Great Ormond Street in 1929.

10. (c) The English language version of this musical opened at the Barbican on a limited three-month residency on 8 October 1985. In 2006, it became the longest-running West End musical in history and at the time of writing is still going strong at the Queen's Theatre.

11. (b) The show featured the first songs Coward had written for his long-term muse and collaborator, Gertrude Lawrence, which helped her star to rise.

12. (c) When Covent Garden was rebuilt in 1809, after being destroyed by fire the previous year, the new gallery was so far up and steeply pitched that audience members could only see the actors' feet and legs. After the national anthem played, angry theatregoers stormed the lower levels of the theatre and 500 soldiers were called out to subdue them. The play that evening was *Macbeth*, the same production that had been disrupted by fire. This story provides yet another example of why *Macbeth* is considered a cursed play in theatrical circles.

13. (a) A 'Save London Theatres' campaign, led by theatre owners with support from Equity and the Musicians' Union, stopped the GLC's redevelopment plans.

14. (c) The Garrick theatre was financed by W. S. Gilbert of Gilbert and Sullivan, who commissioned architects Walter Emden and C. J. Phipps to design the theatre on its less-than-stable site on Charing Cross Road. But the river has not affected the theatre's fortunes—the Grade II listed building, which retains many of its original Victorian features, was purchased by Andrew Lloyd Webber in 2000, and is going strong as part of his group of Really Useful Theatres to this day.

15. (c) A female ghost has been rumoured to haunt the tunnels. The ghost is said to be a Victorian actress who met her end onstage. Fittingly enough, Aldwych is a ghost tube station itself and has not been in use—except as a film and television location—since 1994.

16. (a) After the Restoration of Charles II to the throne, theatres, ich had been banned under Puritan rule, were allowed once more. However, very few were licensed to perform 'serious' drama, and plays had to be approved by a government censor. In London, the Theatre Royal, Drury Lane and Lincoln's Inn Fields (later the Theatre Royal, Covent Garden) were the only two licensed, or 'patent' theatres in London. These were followed by the opening of the Theatre Royal, Haymarket in 1766.

17. (b) From 1737, the time of the first Prime Minister Robert Walpole's Theatrical Licensing Act, until 1968, all plays had to be licensed by the Lord Chamberlain's office before they could appear on the London stage. Three plays produced by the Royal Court in 1968, John Osborne's *A Patriot for Me* and Edward Bond's *Saved* and *Early Morning*, were refused permission to be performed at all. Outrage over the bans led to an end of theatrical censorship. The Soho Theatre, also known for encouraging new writing, did not open until 1969.

18. (b) The Shaftesbury's ceiling collapsed as *Hair* began its 2000th performance, finally closing the show. After this incident, the theatre was almost redeveloped, before a campaign from Equity—and some long-needed repairs—saved the theatre. It reopened with *West Side Story* the following year, and remains known as a home to large-scale musicals.

19. (a) The Apollo Victoria had its interiors redesigned in 1984, to accommodate multilevel race tracks for the roller-skating cast of *Starlight Express* to zip around the stage and through the audience. The tracks were dismantled for the last time after *Starlight Express* closed a revival run in 2002.

20. (b) Below the Phoenix theatre is the Phoenix Artist Club, a louche drinking den covered in decades' worth of headshots and playbills. You're as likely to hear your favourite show tunes as songs from musicals long-forgotten. It's also one of the few places in the West End where starving actors can afford a round, and possibly the only place one can find beer mats (ostensibly for smoking breaks) which read 'I'm out with a fag'.

ROYAL LONDON

1. (a) The Royal Standard is the flag used by the Queen in her capacity as Sovereign of the United Kingdom.

2. (c) In total Buckingham Palace was hit seven times by bombs during the Blitz and the palace chapel was almost entirely destroyed.

3. (c) The Queen Mother lived there from 1953 until her death in 2002. Clarence House is now the official residence of Prince Charles, the Duchess of Cornwall and Princes William and Harry.

4. (b) In 1830, a large monument was erected to the memory of the recently deceased George IV at the junction of Gray's Inn Road, Pentonville Road and what is now Euston Road. It was extremely unpopular, attracting much criticism and derision, and it was demolished only fifteen years later. However the name of King's Cross has survived.

5. (b) The leper hospital, founded in the twelfth century, was dedicated to St. James the Less and was demolished in 1531 to make way for Henry's palace.

(c) The statue is a late-nineteenth-century copy of the original erected in 1712 to mark the completion of the cathedral. Satirists at the time noted the position of the statue of the drink-loving queen in relation to St. Paul's and the local hostelries opposite, one writing, 'Brandy Nan, Brandy Nan / You're left in the lurch / Your face to the gin shop / Your back to the church.'

7. (c) The other events happened at other coronations. Richard II lost his shoe; James II was seen to clutch the crown as it wobbled on his head.

8. (a) Analysis of the hair revealed unexpectedly high levels of arsenic which may be a sign that the king's episodes of madness were a consequence of suffering from the disease porphyria. A pair of Queen Victoria's drawers is kept in the Museum of London. The British Museum has Elizabeth I's purse although it is not, as the word suggests today, a personal bag but an elaborately embroidered holder for the Great Seal which was attached to all official documents.

9. (a) According to one tradition, her husband James I gave Anne the manor of Greenwich as a way of apologising for swearing at her when she accidentally killed one of his dogs while out hunting.

10. (b) George II not only lived at Kensington Palace, he also died there on 25 October 1760 when he suffered a stroke in his toilet while straining to relieve the royal bowels.

11. (a) Prince Frederick was the Commander-in-Chief of the British Army and is remembered as the 'Grand Old Duke of York' in the rhyme who marched his men up the hill and then marched them down again. When he died, he was £2 million in debt.

12. (b) The Bruton Street address was the London home of her maternal grandparents, the 14th Earl and Countess of Strathmore. The Duke of Edinburgh was born on Corfu; Prince Michael of Kent made his first appearance in the world in Buckinghamshire.

13. (a) Albert was, of course, one of the prime movers of the Great Exhibition and it is fitting that he should hold the catalogue for it on the statue. The Albert Memorial also includes two groups of allegorical sculptures—one of the four continents of Africa, America, Asia and Europe and one of figures representing Agriculture, Commerce, Engineering and Manufacture.

14. (b) The Dymokes were hereditary holders of the office of King's or Queen's Champion and performed their duties at every coronation from that of Richard II to that of George IV. The story that a Jacobite swordsman, disguised as an old woman, stood up at the coronation of William III and challenged the reigning Dymoke to a duel in Hyde Park the following day is, sadly, apocryphal.

15. (c) St. George's was designed by Nicholas Hawksmoor who was the architect for five other churches in the capital, including Christ Church, Spitalfields and St. Alfege's, Greenwich. The statue shows the king in Roman dress.

16. (a) In 1848 the ruling classes became very agitated at the prospect of the working class Chartists marching through the streets of London to present a giant petition to Parliament demanding political reform. Napoleon was one of those who volunteered to act as a special constable to combat revolutionary upheaval which, in the event, didn't take place.

7. (c) The Dutch king made the decision to move from Whitehall shortly after taking the throne in the Glorious Revolution.

18. (b) Defeated in battle and with his kingdom in the process of being dismantled, Cetewayo was allowed to visit London. He also had an audience with Queen Victoria at Osborne House on the Isle of Wight.

19. (a) The fire destroyed very nearly all the straggling buildings of the palace.

20. (c) The Square was originally laid out in the 1670s and named after Charles II. The statue of the king has had a chequered career and was removed from the square during alterations in the 1870s. For a time it stood in the garden of a house in Harrow belonging to W. S. Gilbert but was returned to Soho Square in 1938.

FOLKLORE AND CUSTOMS

1. (b) One of a family of dancers and clowns, Joseph Grimaldi made his first appearance on stage in 1781 when he was less than two years old and went on to become the archetypal clown of English pantomime. The Clowns' Services began in 1946 at St. James's, Islington, the church in whose grounds Grimaldi was buried, but St. James's was demolished and the service transferred to Dalston in 1959. Since 1967 the clowns who attend the service have been allowed to dress in their full motley and makeup so the pews are filled with white-faced men with red noses and baggy pants, giving thanks to the man who is still regarded as the father of English clowning.

2. (a) In the fourteenth century a knight named Sir Robert Knollys built a footbridge to connect two properties he owned on either side of Seething Lane. Building the bridge breached city regulations and he was fined. However, in recognition of his recent military service in France, the fine imposed was an undemanding one: he, and his descendants, had to present a red rose from his garden to the lord mayor every Midsummer's Day. The ceremony still continues. Every 24 June churchwardens at All Hallows-by-the-Tower carry a red rose to the Mansion House on an altar cushion where it is presented to the Lord Mayor together with a bouquet of roses for the Lady Mayoress.

3. (a) Sweeney Todd, the Demon Barber of Fleet Street, who cut the throats of his customers and turned them into meat pies, is often described as a real historical character, but there is very little evidence that he was anything other than the product of a penny dreadful writer's lurid imagination.

4. (b) The duel (over a woman) was allegedly fought around 1685 in meadows long covered over by Montague Street. Both brothers were killed but the impressions of their feet, made as they walked away from one another before turning to fire their pistols, were supposedly visible for more than a century afterwards.

5. (c) At least seven centuries old, the Ceremony of the Keys is a nightly ritual in which the Chief Yeoman Warder, with an escort, undertakes the locking of several gates to the Tower. At the entrance to the Bloody Tower there is a formal challenge from a sentry ('Who comes there?'), which is answered by the Chief Warder and the ceremony is brought to a conclusion.

b) Boudicca. The myth that Boudicca and her daughters re buried under platform 10 at King's Cross station probably originated in the 1930s when a writer called Lewis Spence claimed that the battle between her army and the Romans took place in the valley where King's Cross and St. Pancras stations now stand. Although Spence never suggested that Boudicca was buried there, the idea that she was seems to have caught people's imaginations.

7. (b) Every Shrove Tuesday since 1753 the pupils of Westminster School have been allowed a minute of licensed mayhem during which they fight to get hold of pieces of a 'pancake' thrown over the bar that once separated two parts of the school. The 'pancake' is actually made largely of horsehair.

8. (b) Perhaps unsurprisingly, the story first appears in a 1632 book called *Histriomastix* by the Puritan William Prynne who was violently against what he saw as the frivolity and licentiousness of the theatre.

9. (c) Henry VI died in the Wakefield Tower on 21 May 1471. He may have died a natural death but it is just as likely that Edward IV, who had deposed and imprisoned him, arranged to have him murdered.

10. (b) The Dyers and the Vintners are now the only owners of Thames swans other than the Crown. The Dyers mark theirs with a nick on one side of the beak; the Vintners mark theirs with a nick on each side of the beak. The pub name 'The Swan with Two Necks', in which 'necks' is a corruption of 'nicks', refers to this practice.

11. (c) The feast was held on 1 May each year at her house in Portman Square. According to a story told by many writers, including Dickens, her generosity was a result of finding her own child working as a chimney sweep after he had been kidnapped.

12. (b) The ceremony dates back to the Middle Ages but, since 1887, the poor widows, thanks to a bequest from a gentleman named Joshua Whitehead Butterworth, have also received an extra treat in the shape of small coins to accompany their buns.

13. (a) According to the twelfth-century writer Geoffrey of Monmouth, 'Belinus caused to be constructed a gateway of extraordinary workmanship, which in his time the citizens called Billingsgate, from his own name'.

14. (a) Robert Baddeley was an eighteenth-century actor. When he died in November 1794, he left property to found a home for 'decayed' actors and also £3 per annum to provide wine and a specially baked cake in the green room of Drury Lane Theatre every Twelfth Night. The ceremony of cutting (and eating) the Baddeley cake has remained a regular tradition.

15. (c) Created in the 1920s by the sculptor Basil Ionides, Kaspar the Savoy Cat is a three-foot-high, black wooden cat which is used in the dining rooms of the hotel when thirteen people sit down to a meal. The unlucky number is brought up to fourteen by Kaspar who is placed at the table, with a napkin around his neck, and provided with each of the dishes in turn.

16. (a) The ceremony takes place every year at the Royal Courts of Justice when six horseshoes and sixty-one nails are counted out by the City Solicitor and given to a judicial officer called the

een's Remembrancer. This is the 'quit rent' or token lease
aid for a forge which used to stand in the Strand, approximately
on the present site of Australia House. The custom dates back to
the thirteenth century.

17. (c) Thomas Doggett was a Dublin-born actor and theatre
manager who, on 1 August 1715, sponsored a race for young
watermen to be rowed along the Thames to commemorate the
accession of George I to the British throne. It has continued ever
since. The winner is presented with an orange-coloured coat,
knee breeches, silk stockings and cap, and a round silver badge,
some nine inches in diameter, which bears an image of the white
horse of Hanover on it.

18. (a) In the mid-1930s a ghostly bus was regularly seen
careering along the roads of Ladbroke Grove in the early hours of
the morning. The ghost of a bear used to haunt Cheyne Walk in
Chelsea in the late nineteenth century and there have, of course,
been countless tales of long-dead Egyptians prowling through
the rooms of the British Museum.

19. (b) Since 1864, some hardy souls in the Serpentine
Swimming Club have competed in a 100-yard swimming race on
Christmas Day. In 1904 J. M. Barrie presented the Peter Pan Cup
as a prize for the winner.

20. (c) Sir John Gayer was Lord Mayor in 1646. As a young man,
he had been shipwrecked on the coast of Africa and had come
face to face with a lion. He had dropped to his knees in prayer
when it approached. The lion, after sniffing him and prowling
around him for a while, had sloped off without harming him,
proof, in Sir John's mind, of the efficacy of prayer. He left money

in his will so that a sermon could be preached annually in St. Katharine Cree.

DRINKERS' LONDON

1. (a) In 1514 the guild became the Worshipful Company of Innholders.

2. (c) Its namesake provided the basis for Miss Havisham in *Great Expectations*. The original Dirty Dick was a young dandy called Nathaniel Bentley who owned a warehouse on Leadenhall Street. On the eve of a great feast to celebrate his wedding, his bride-to-be died. Bentley shut the dining room up, leaving all the food set out to rot and decay. Grief-stricken, he himself gave up washing and neglected his appearance for the rest of his days. 'It is of no use; if I wash my hands today', he argued, 'they will be dirty again tomorrow'. A poem based on his squalid life entitled 'Dirty Old Man' appeared in *Household Words*, the magazine Dickens edited some years before the novelist penned *Great Expectations.*

3. (a) It was a quirk of the licensing laws then that pubs in Holborn had to close at 10:30, while those in Marylebone could remain open until eleven. The boundary line between the two boroughs ran down the middle of Charlotte Street. Thirsty writers like Dylan Thomas and Julian Maclaren Ross would therefore pelt down the road to gain an extra half an hour's drinking time.

4. (b) Officially called The York Minster, it was always referred to as 'the French pub' before finally being renamed. The future esident Charles De Gaulle was among those French exiles who eat a path there during the war. The writer John Mortimer once maintained that visiting it was cheaper than paying the fare to Paris.

5. (c) The Major was landlord of the Duke from 1938 until he died in 1964. One former customer described him as 'an irritable but sometimes generous man whose whisky intake was formidable'. His dog, a large bloodhound named 'The Colonel', was a fixture of the pub. The animal was so ferocious-looking that it was once hired by a film company and appeared in a big screen outing of *The Hound of the Baskervilles*.

6. (b) *Private Eye*'s famous fortnightly lunches continue to be held in an upstairs room of the pub. At Balon's retirement party in 2006, the magazine's former editor Richard Ingrams paid tribute to the landlord by saluting him as: 'The only man grumpier than me'. His autobiography, fittingly, was entitled *You're Barred, You Bastards!*

7. (c) In the 1970s, it became the pub of choice for the staff and writers of the poet Ian Hamilton's *New Review*, whose office was at 11 Greek Street. Ian McEwan, Julian Barnes and Martin Amis were among the aspiring literary stars to be found in the Pillars back then.

8. (a) Since the fourteenth century, Ely Place has been the London residence of the Bishops of Ely and as such is part of the Bishop's Cambridgeshire dominions.

9. (c) A cottage once stood on the site occupied by the pub. According to legend it belonged to an old widow whose son—a sailor—was due to arrive home on Good Friday. She put a hot cross bun aside for him but he never returned. Each year she kept a bun, and the ritual was subsequently taken up by the pub after her death.

10. (b) Opened in 1663, it was one of the few taverns in the City of London to escape the blaze.

11. (a) The notorious 'hanging judge' was trying to follow his former master the Catholic James II who had fled to France after the Glorious Revolution of 1688 The Wapping steps were where fishermen from Ramsgate used to unload and sell their wares, hence the pub's name. Jeffreys is reputed to have watched the hangings he handed down carried out on the nearby Execution Dock from the balcony of another famous Wapping hostelry, the Prospect of Whitby. Jeffreys himself escaped the hangman's noose, dying in custody in the Tower of London instead.

12. (a) According to legend, the highwayman's father was a former landlord of the pub and Turpin was a frequent visitor to it. The ghostly hoof beats of Turpin's horse Black Bess are said to be heard galloping across the car park on cold wintery nights.

13. (a) Built in 1872 and named after Queen Victoria's fourth daughter, the pub is a Grade II listed building. It boasts original interior decorative tile work by the celebrated Victorian firm W. B. Simpson of Clapham. At one time, the ornate glass cisterns in the gentlemen's lavatories were said to have sported live goldfish.

14. (c) While London's other great wholesale markets, Covent Garden for fruit and vegetable and Billingsgate for fish, moved to ew sites in the 1970s and 80s, Smithfield meat market remains n its grand Victorian home on Charterhouse Street.

15. (a) Situated at the top of a narrow flight of stairs at 41 Dean Street, The Colony Room Club was virtually a second home to Francis Bacon. Belcher allowed the painter to drink for free and paid him £10 to bring clients in. In more recent years Damien Hirst, Tracey Emin and Kate Moss have all been regulars.

16. (a) It had already been rebuilt after being destroyed in a fire that swept through Southwark in 1676.

17. (b) Built in 1520, it was a popular haunt of smugglers and, later, Charles Dickens and the painter James Abbott McNeill Whistler. Its current name derives from a ship that traded between London and the North Yorkshire fishing town of Whitby.

18. (a) Members of the club included Ernest Dowson, Francis Thompson and Arthur Symons. In earlier times, Samuel Johnson and James Boswell are also said to have quaffed at the Cheese.

19. (a) He fled the intense heat of the blaze on a boat on the river and sought shelter in 'a little alehouse on bankside ... and there watched the fire grow'. The original pub was itself rebuilt after a fire in 1676.

20. (b) Ray and Dave Davies were Muswell Hill locals. The pub is name-checked in the Kinks song 'Fortes Green'.

WARTIME LONDON

1. (c) The picture palaces were by no means safe destinations during the Blitz, yet admissions increased continually through the war, reaching an all-time peak in 1946.

2. (b) The elephants were evacuated to Whipsnade and the poisonous snakes were chloroformed rather than risk their escape into Regents Park should the reptile house take a hit.

3. (a) You might think the risk of sudden death ought to focus thoughts on the ever after, even among the young, but no, they were all off to the movies instead.

4. (a) (b) and **(c)** All three predate the war, the earliest being an alternative name for a skittering insect more often known as the antlion How it became transferred to an unmanned plane is unclear.

5. (c) Crooner Bowlly died outside his Jermyn Street flat when a parachute bomb exploded— his decision to return home from an engagement in Wycombe proved fatal. Snakehips was the resident bandleader at the Café de Paris, where eighty people, including his entire band, died after a direct hit. Edgington, Spike Milligan's comrade-in-arms, survived the sharp end of the war to play on the Goon Show years later.

6. (b) Many concert halls were closed down during the war and Hess's concerts were seen as embodying defiance of the Blitz. She was made a Dame of the British Empire in 1941 in recognition of her work in raising morale.

7. (b) Many other entertainment and sports venues found new r the duration. The All-England Lawn Tennis and Croquet at Wimbledon, for example, was used to raise vegetables.

. (a) Near to the American church, Eisenhower's command centre has long been used as a secure storage space.

9. (c) The child of German Jewish refugees, Springer was born underground after his mother went into labour in the deep level shelter at Highgate.

10. (a) Tired of taking a pounding from the Luftwaffe while the West End remained relatively unscathed, the Cockneys were fuming.

11. (c) Orwell's (rented) basement flat in Kilburn was hit by a V1 flying bomb, while Greene's Queen Anne house in Clapham and Woolf's townhouse in Mecklenburgh Square were destroyed from above.

12. (b) Shut in the twenties for structural reasons, the rebuilding of Waterloo Bridge was so protracted that it didn't start until 1939 and wasn't officially completed until war's end, though it was partially open by 1942.

13. (a) Some Londoners complained about the American occupation of Mayfair.

14. (a) Mickey Mouse gas masks were manufactured in bright primary colours and were intended to be less distressing to wear for young children.

15. (c) This was quite a lot of money at the time.

16. (b) Fifteen years old, he pinched the bottom of a soldier's girlfriend in the crush.

17. (a) The facilities were used to help manufacture heavy Halifax bombers. Though when Albert Durrant, LT's chief engineer and the brains behind the legendary Routemaster, was seconded to tank design, the legendary Centurion model his team devised was partly tested at the bus works.

18. (c) It was called the *Swiss Cottager*.

19. (a) Seven people were killed in the blast.

20. (a) Miller was due to stay in Sloane Court but had to take shelter from a flying bomb attack. Two days later Miller and his group were taken out to Bedford. A week later Sloane Court was hit and twenty-six people were killed.

LITERARY LONDON

1. (b) All three writers spent periods of their life in London. Rousseau lived in Buckingham Street and Chiswick; Rimbaud, together with his lover Paul Verlaine, stayed in what is now Royal College Street in Camden and at several other addresses in the city. Only Voltaire lodged in Maiden Lane.

2. (c) The Sherlock Holmes opened under its present name in the 1950s and includes a replica of the great detective's apartment at 221B Baker Street which was first put on display at the Festival of Britain in 1951.

o) The statue is the work of the nineteenth-century Scottish sculptor Sir John Steell and was the gift of a founding member of The Burns Society of London. An earlier casting of the same statue can be found in Central Park, New York.

4. (a) In *Gulliver's Travels* the hero lives at three London addresses before taking a ship from Bristol on the fateful voyage that landed him in Lilliput.

5. (b) He had left his lodgings in Poland Street, Soho, now marked with a blue plaque, and walked the half mile to the Square without awakening.

6. (c) In 1903, five years before the publication of *The Wind in the Willows*, Grahame was lucky to survive a bizarre incident at the Bank when a disturbed young man named Robinson pulled out a gun and fired three shots at him.

7. (b) It was while he was living at the house in Gough Square that he compiled his famous dictionary. The Dickens House is in Doughty Street; Carlyle's House is in Cheyne Row, Chelsea. Both are open to the public.

8. (b) Lamb was born in the Inner Temple where his father worked as a lawyer's clerk and there is a plaque to mark the site of his birthplace.

9. (a) The theft is witnessed by a shocked Oliver Twist who ends up charged with the crime himself.

10. (b) He accepts a bet from his fellow members who believe that it cannot be done.

11. (c) Frieda Strindberg opened The Cave of the Golden Ca~
1912.

12. (a) The George and Vulture still exists in Castle Court just off
Lombard Street.

13. (c) Barrie, who died in 1937, stipulated that future earnings
from *Peter Pan* should go to the hospital which now has a Barrie
Wing, a Peter Pan Ward and a bronze statue of the boy who
wouldn't grow up at its entrance.

14. (b) The chemical laboratory at Bart's was, according to
Arthur Conan Doyle in his 1887 novel *A Study in Scarlet*, the
location for the first meeting between Sherlock Holmes and Dr.
Watson. A plaque recording the encounter can be seen in the
hospital's museum just inside the Henry VIII gate.

15. (a) The author of *Tristram Shandy* died in poverty in lodgings
in Old Bond Street in 1768. According to one story, the two
men who laid out his corpse stole his gold cufflinks by way of
payment.

16. (a) The assault took place close to the Lamb and Flag pub in
what is now Rose Street

17. (c) Between 1807 and 1816, the house was occupied by the
bank Austen, Maunde and Tilson of which Jane Austen's brother
Henry was a director. She stayed here with Henry on visits to
London in 1813 and 1814.

18. (a) Chandler visited London for long holidays after the death
of his wife Cissie and was clearly seeking solace for her loss.

, The Cock Lane Ghost was one of the sensations of ~eenth-century London.

~0. (a) 27 Wimpole Street exists and is a doctors' surgery. The address 27A Wimpole Street does not exist and never did, outside the imagination of George Bernard Shaw. Dracula, under the guise of Count De Ville, buys a crumbling mansion at 347 Piccadilly; Mr. Pooter and his wife live in suburban splendour at The Laurels, Brickfield Terrace, Holloway.

LONDON BUILDINGS

1. (a) Leighton House was the home of Frederic, Lord Leighton, the Victorian artist and President of the Royal Academy. It is now a museum and gallery and the Arab hall, designed to display Leighton's collection of Islamic tiles, is its most remarkable sight for visitors.

2. (a) The concert hall was built in 1901 by the famous firm of piano manufacturers, Bechstein, next to their London showrooms. During the First World War, German firms like Bechstein were under constant threat and the hall, together with the company's other assets, was sold for a fraction of its true value, to Debenham's. The hall re-opened under the name of Wigmore Hall in 1917.

3. (b) There has been an inn on the site since medieval times, although the present buildings date only from the seventeenth century. There were once galleries on three sides of the courtyard but two were demolished when the railways came to the area.

4. (a) Sir Edward Watkin was an MP and railway tycoon who proposed building a tower in Wembley Park that would rise higher than its Parisian counterpart and accommodate restaurants, theatres, a ballroom and a Turkish bath. It only reached 200 feet in height before the money ran out. The project was abandoned and the tower dynamited out of existence in 1907. The remains of Watkin's tower were rediscovered recently when the foundations of the new Wembley stadium were being dug.

5. (b) The Crystal Palace was transported from its original site in Hyde Park to Sydenham after the Great Exhibition of 1851. Despite the efforts of nearly a hundred fire engines and more than a thousand firemen, it was reduced to a smouldering ruin of twisted iron and melted glass in the 1936 fire.

6. (a) The dummy houses were created when the Underground was constructed in the 1860s. The original, steam-driven underground trains needed open air stretches of track to release fumes and the gap behind the house facades in Leinster Gardens provided one such place.

7. (b) The unabashed nudity of Gill's sculptural reliefs offended some people and, in Parliament, one MP called them 'objectionable to public morals and decency'. The story that Gill was obliged to reduce the size of Ariel's genitalia in order to deflect criticism has often been told but may well be apocryphal.

8. (c) Twickenham is the home of the English Rugby Union. In 1906, a rugby enthusiast and property developer named William Williams was given the job of finding a site for a new stadium. The land he bought was once a market garden and was originally

ered such a poor choice for a rugby ground that it was
vely dubbed 'Billy Williams' Cabbage Patch'.

. **(b)** The facade of the house, an extremely rare survival
of a timber-framed house from before the Great Fire, is on
display in the Victoria and Albert museum. It originally stood in
Bishopsgate on the site of what is now Liverpool Street Station
and was donated to the museum when the station was enlarged
in 1890.

10. (c) The grasshopper was the crest of Sir Thomas Gresham,
the Elizabethan entrepreneur who founded what became the
Royal Exchange.

11. (b) Rahere was certainly a courtier of Henry I and may well
have been his jester. He fell sick while on a pilgrimage abroad
and vowed to build a hospital and dedicate it to St. Bartholomew
if he survived to return to London.

12. (a) Ministry of Sound was founded by the entrepreneur
James Palumbo and the DJ Justin Berkmann in 1991 in order to
create a London club devoted to U.S. house music. It is now a
worldwide brand.

13. (a) The ten-storey pagoda was one of several buildings in the
Gardens designed by Sir William Chambers, official architect to
Princess Augusta, Dowager Princess of Wales and the mother of
George III.

14. (a) During the Second World War the exiled King of
Yugoslavia was living at Claridge's when his wife gave birth to
a son and heir. Churchill declared the suite where he was living

Yugoslav territory for a day to ensure that the child would right to the throne.

15. (c) The present Central Criminal Court or Old Bailey building opened in the Edwardian era and stands on the site of the infamous Newgate Prison. Answer (a) is the motto of the BBC which is inscribed on Broadcasting House: Answer (b), which means 'Everything for Everybody Everywhere', is the motto of Harrods.

16. (b) So named because of its shape, the giant tower, the sixth tallest building in London, was designed by Norman Foster.

17. (b) A quadriga is a type of Roman war chariot. The Wellington Arch was at one time surmounted by a huge equestrian statue of the Iron Duke, but the present piece was placed there in 1912. 'The Angel of Christian Charity' is one of the names given to the statue in Piccadilly Circus more commonly known as 'Eros'; an original cast of Rodin's 'The Burghers of Calais' stands in Victoria Tower Gardens.

18. (a) Mithraism was a particularly popular cult among Roman soldiers. Other finds from the excavation, which can be seen in the Museum of London and the British Museum, include a head of Mithras and a statue of the god engaged in the ritual slaying of a bull.

19. (b) The building, designed by William Wilkins, met with much criticism when it was opened in the 1830s and was compared to a cruet stand, presumably because of the assortment of cupolas with which it is crowned.

was Morris's home from 1879 until his death in 1896
named it after the Oxfordshire village where he had
ously lived. In 1891, he founded the Kelmscott Press in
mmersmith to produce fine editions of his own works and of
ne classics.

ROADS AND RIVERS

1. (b) The name dates back to the eleventh century although the story about the fighting knights is not recorded until much later.

2. (a) The game, although the participants in it pretend otherwise, has no real rules and it progresses through improvisation and word association on the part of the panellists until one of them randomly announces, 'Mornington Crescent' and brings it to an end.

3. (a) The plan for the tunnel was published by Marc Brunel, and authorised in Parliament in 1823. Work on the project was not completed until 1843. In the 1860s it was converted into a railway tunnel for trains on the East London Railway, and it carries trains on the East London underground line to this day.

4. (a) It was once known as Duke Street but was renamed in 1894 because there were so many other streets in London of that name.

5. (b) Thousands were also made homeless. Water poured into Millbank and over the Embankment near Charing Cross, and part of the Chelsea Embankment collapsed.

6. (c) A pickadil was a type of stiff lace collar popular in t
seventeenth century. It is thought that the street is named
a house built in 1612 on what was then open country to the w
of the city by a wealthy tailor named Robert Baker. The house
was mockingly nicknamed Piccadilly House after the pickadils
that had made Baker's fortune, and the name stuck.

7. (b) There were once many methane-powered lamps but this is
one of very few to survive. The sewer that provides the methane
takes much of its waste from the nearby Savoy Hotel.

8. (a) Though diving from Tower Bridge was a favourite feat of
Victorian circus performers and sportsmen.

9. (b) Aldwych was the heart of the old Anglo-Saxon city of
Loudenweg which stretched from Fleet Street to roughly where
the National Gallery is now.

10. (a) It was given this name because the River Tyburn once
flowed across it and because it led past the gallows at Tyburn.
It began to be called Oxford Street in the second half of the
eighteenth century because much of the land around it was
owned by the Earl of Oxford.

11. (a) Hamilton had part of the river diverted so that it
passed through the garden of their retreat at Merton Place in
Wimbledon.

12. (a) Deptford was where both the playwright Christopher
Marlowe was murdered and Lord Daubeny bested the Kentish
Rebels for King Henry VII in 1497.

he street was probably named after a man called
e, while it's replacement is thought to hail from the
holder rather than the Puritan poet. Johnson had lived and
rked on the street himself as a struggling writer.

14. (c) Its name derived from a hangman's noose, a Devil's
Neckinger, as pirates were executed on a wharf where this river,
which runs through Bermondsey, met the Thames.

15. (c) Today the epicentre of London's gay life, it was the
meeting place for çontinental exiles for many years. The French
poets and lovers Arthur Rimbaud and Paul Verlaine frequented
the Hibernia Tavern on Old Compton Street during their sojourn
to London in 1872.

16. (b) There are over 120 different aquatic species in the Thames.

17. (c) According to Stow, the area, once a moat that bounded
the City wall, got its name 'from that in old time, when the same
lay open, much filth (conveyed forth of the City), especially dead
dogges were there laid or cast'.

18. (b) Paille maille was a French game popular in the
seventeenth century and played on this long, wide avenue back
in the day.

19. (c) Rising in West Hampstead and flowing down to Hyde
Park and onto Knightsbridge out to the Thames, the Westbourne
was dammed up to form the Serpentine in the 1730s.

20. (a) This river, which takes its name from the Anglo-Saxon
for a tidal inlet, still flows beneath Farringdon Road today.

SHOPS AND SHOPPING

1. (a) A branch of the Whole Foods chain now has the run of ground floor of this lovely Art Deco building. The original frieze on the front of the building, depicting such totems of modernity as aeroplanes and streamlined steam trains, is still visible.

2. (c) Biba moved into the old seven-storey Derry and Toms building in September 1973. Designer Barbara Hulanicki and her husband Simon Fitzsimon spent over £1M refurbishing this Art Deco department store, creating a fantasy retail palace with a roof garden and a pink marble floored Rainbow Room restaurant and concert hall. Performers who appeared there ranged from the New York Dolls to The Wombles, from Liberace to The Bay City Rollers. But the expansion proved a costly failure and they were forced to close two years later.

3. (a) Charles Henry Harrod set up as a wholesale grocer in Stepney in 1834. To escape the squalor of the East End and to capitalise on trade to the Great Exhibition of 1851 in nearby Hyde Park, he moved west in 1849, taking a small shop in the new district of Knightsbridge where Harrods has remained ever since.

4. (a) Her shop is at 40 Brushfield Street, Spitalfields Market. As Winterson told *Good Housekeeping* magazine: "The ground floor had first opened as a shop in 1805. My building had been a fruit importer, and the place was pasted with ancient posters urging me to 'Eat More Oranges' ".

5. (c) Three years earlier, John Logie Baird had given one of the first demonstrations of a television broadcast in the store.

ce ubiquitous in the City of London, the bowler was
ntly created by Lock & Co. for a gentleman called Coker
was looking for a practical curved hat that his country
ate's gamekeepers could wear without getting snagged by
branches.

7. (b) Beyond the realms of fiction, Stanfords also supplied Dr.
Livingstone, Amy Johnson, Cecil Rhodes, Florence Nightingale,
Sir Wilfred Thesiger and Michael Palin with maps for their
various journeys. It also provided employment for the *Carry On*
star Kenneth Williams, who trained as a draftsman at Stanfords
before his acting career took off.

8. (b) Fortnum worked as footman to Queen Anne and was
charged with replacing the candles from the candelabras each
evening. He made enough cash from selling the spare wax to
set up a shop in partnership with a Mr. Hugh Mason in Piccadilly
in 1707.

9. (b) Established by Benjamin Harvey, the business passed
onto his daughter in 1820 on the understanding that she go into
partnership with a Colonel Nichols, selling luxury and Oriental
goods alongside the linens.

10. (c) Established in 1797 and moved to its current site at 187
Piccadilly in 1801, the shop counted the Duke of Wellington as
one of its most loyal early customers.

11. (a) Designed in 1936 by Joseph Emberton, this striking
modernist building at 203 Piccadilly is now home to
Waterstone's and is the largest bookshop in Britain.

12. (b) Other famous clients since the firm was establis.
1885 have included Ian Fleming, Michael Caine, David Niv
Winston Churchill.

13. (a) Her request was refused. The Fuhrer argued that, if the
books were bad for Germans, then they would be bad for the
British too.

14. (c) The man behind the Amstrad personal computer and star
of *The Apprentice*, started out as a teenager flogging beetroots
at this market. There had been a market on this site since the
seventeenth century. Although the lane itself was renamed
Middlesex Street in 1830, the market continues to be known by
the name it originally acquired from the secondhand clothing
dealers who first clustered there to sell their wares.

15. (a) Leigh Underhill opened the first antique shop in this
then relatively down-at-the-heels Georgian back street in the
early 1960s. The regular market was subsequently established
by local music shop owner John Peyton, who led a successful
campaign to prevent the council from demolishing the street and
building flats on the site.

16. (a) Until Stephen and his partner Bill Franks took out a
lease on a shop at Number 5 in 1956, Carnaby Street was an
undistinguished back alley in Soho, known only for a tobacconist
called Inverwick's. By 1964, Stephen had eleven men's clothing
outlets on Carnaby Street alone, and branches on the King's
Road, Old Compton Street and in South Kensington.

17. (b) Quant, who helped make Chelsea hip and named and
popularized the miniskirt, opened this boutique at Markham

...A King's Road, with her husband Alexander Plunkett-
... 1955. In its heady early days Quant would often be
...g dresses at night to sell for the following morning, while
...husband presided over a basement bistro called Alexander's.

18. (a) John Lydon, soon re-christened Johnny Rotten, auditioned for the Sex Pistols in the shop, singing along to Alice Cooper's 'Eighteen' on SEX's 1950s jukebox. The site remains home to the World's End boutique Westwood opened in 1980.

19. (a) Despite claims on the building itself to the contrary, it was not the model for Charles Dickens's own Old Curiosity Shop, which most believe stood on Fetter Lane and had been pulled down before his tale was even published. This former dairy, now a handmade shoe emporium, is the only remaining building of the old Clare Market, cleared when Kingsway was laid out at the end of the nineteenth century.

20. (b) Horace George Raynor visited Whiteley in his office to demand that he be given a job. When Whiteley refused, Raynor shot him. At his trial, he alleged that the department store owner was his real father but would not acknowledge him. Raynor was first sentenced to hang, but this was later commuted to life imprisonment.

LONDON CHURCHES

1. (c) According to Oleg Gordievsky, a KGB agent who defected to the West, the Oratory contained a 'dead letter box' or agreed location where spies could leave messages for one another. He also claimed there was another such site near a statue of

St. Francis of Assisi in the grounds of the nearby Holy
Church.

2. (c) After his execution, Raleigh's head was presented to
his wife who had it embalmed. His body was buried in St.
Margaret's. Thirty years later, after her death, his head was
buried in the same church but not in the same place as the body.

3. (a) Legend has it that a local Fleet Street baker named
William Rich modelled the wedding cakes he created on the
three-tiered spire of St. Bride's. Other bakers followed suit and
now the traditional wedding cake always takes that shape.

4. (b) Bligh's tomb at St. Mary's (now deconsecrated and
transformed into the Museum of Garden History) can still be
seen. The inscription on it makes no mention of the Mutiny on
the Bounty for which Bligh is now best remembered.

5. (b) Like St. Christopher, St. Botolph was known as a patron
saint of travellers and, for this reason, four churches near gates
in the city walls were dedicated to him. Three of them—St.
Botolph Aldersgate, St. Botolph's Aldgate and St. Botolph-
without-Bishopsgate—survive.

6. (c) The architect Inigo Jones was told by his patron, the
Earl of Bedford, that he had little money to spend and that
the finished church should be 'no better than a barn'. Jones is
reported to have replied to the Earl, 'Well, then, you shall have
the handsomest barn in England'.

7. (b) Chad Varah had just been appointed rector of St. Stephen
Walbrook when he founded the Samaritans. The first telephone

to receive calls from the distressed and potentially
was in the crypt of the church.

) Also known as the Kitchener Memorial Chapel, it was
dedicated in 1925 to the memory of the famous soldier of Empire
and the servicemen who died in the First World War.

9. (b) All Souls, which was consecrated in 1824, was part of
Nash's large-scale development of Regent's Park and Regent
Street.

10. (c) The church took its name from a nearby street which, in
turn, owed its name to that of the French town. The name recalls
the medieval wine trade between England and France as did
that of St. Martin Vintry, a church that once stood close to St.
Michael Paternoster Royal but was destroyed during the Great
Fire and never rebuilt.

11. (a) Remembered as a traitor by Americans, Benedict Arnold
lived in London for the last ten years of his life. He and his wife
and his daughter were all buried in the crypt of what was their
local parish church.

12. (b) Disraeli's family was Jewish, but his father quarrelled
with the authorities at the Bevis Marks Synagogue and brought
the twelve-year-old Benjamin to St. Andrew's to be christened
as an act of protest. Because he did so, his son was able to enter
Parliament in 1837, more than twenty years before Jews were
finally allowed to take seats there.

13. (a) The most notable features of the church are the caryatids
(female figures acting as architectural supports) on the porch

which are directly copied from those in Athens. Their sculp.
Charles Rossi, originally made the figures too tall. Slices had t
be taken out of their midriffs before they could fit into the space
provided for them.

14. (b) Newton was rector of St. Mary Woolnoth in Lombard
Street from 1780 until his death in 1807.

15. (a) John Stow was one of London's first historians. After
his death in 1605, his widow arranged for a memorial effigy of
him, holding a quill pen in his hand, to be placed in St. Andrew
Undershaft. On the anniversary of his death each year a service
is held and the quill pen is replaced with a new one.

16. (b) Rugby. As a schoolboy at Rugby School in the 1820s,
William Webb Ellis supposedly created a new form of football
when he picked up the ball during a game and ran with it. In
later life he became a clergyman and was rector of St. Clement
Danes in the 1850s. Sadly, the story of his invention of rugby is
almost certainly nothing more than that—a story invented by an
imaginative contemporary a few years after Webb Ellis's death.

17. (c) The story goes that the Queen, when asked by the
architect what design she would prefer, kicked over a footstool
and told him to build the church like that. The four towers of St.
John's supposedly resemble the four upturned legs of a stool.
Sadly, the tale is apocryphal but the nickname endures.

18. (b) The young woman responded to his advances by taking
several pins out of her pocket and preparing to jab him with
them.

The church claims to be able to trace its origins back to
\D.

0. (a) Dickens gave the church the nickname of St. Ghastly
Grim in an essay in his book *The Uncommercial Traveller*, in
reference to the stone skulls and bones which are carved into
the gateway leading into the churchyard.

LONDON TRANSPORT

1. (a) His first horse bus ran from Paddington to Bank. The fare
was 1 shilling, including the use of newspapers.

2. (b) The nickname was quickly adopted by the line's owners.
This move was criticised by *Railway* magazine which grumbled
that it was a 'gutter title' and not what they 'expected of a
railway company'.

3. (b) The name was eventually rejected because the board of
London Transport felt it sounded 'too bullying'. The Londoner
was the title of the double-decker bus unveiled in 1970 as the
Routemaster's initial successor.

4. (c) The idea of numbered routes came from the German
guidebook firm Baedeker and was adopted in London by the
Vanguard bus company. The first numbered bus, the 4, ran from
Gospel Oak to Putney station on 23 April 1906.

5. (c) The station was Beck's local. The map can be found on the
southbound platform. In 2006, his map was voted the second
best design of the twentieth century in the BBC's Great British
Design Quest.

6. (a) Its 'moving staircase' was installed in October 1911. According to urban legend, a one-legged man called Bumper Harris was hired to ride up and down the escalator to reassure passengers too nervous to use it.

7. (b) The line, opened by the London and South Western Railway in 1898, travels between just two stations, Waterloo and Bank.

8. (b) The first electric trams appeared on London's streets in 1901 following on from horse-drawn trams which were introduced in 1861. On that final run, the tram's journey time was extended by almost three hours as crowds of cheering Londoners surrounded it along various stages of the route from Woolwich to New Cross.

9. (b) A kind of winged-dragon, the wyvern was the heraldic emblem of the Midland Railway company, who funded this superlative example of neo-Gothic architecture by George Gilbert Scott in the 1860s.

10. (a) Restrictions on further building in the area, ushered in by the establishment of Hampstead Garden Suburb in 1907, made the station unviable. It was therefore abandoned before it was finished. Frank Pick did, however, live not far away in Golders Green. There is a blue plaque on his former home at 15 Wildwood Road.

11. (c) The funeral trains carrying mourners and cadavers left from a special station at 121 Westminster Bridge Road, just outside the main Waterloo terminus. The station contained a mortuary and a private chapel of rest. It was hit by a German

n the Blitz in 1941 and not rebuilt, though much of its
rate facade is still intact.

2. (c) Its designer Charles Holden had visited the Russian
capital with a team of engineers from London Transport in the
1930s. A reciprocal trip was made to London soon afterwards by
their counterparts on the Moscow Metro. This arrangement was
obviously fruitful enough for the Soviets, as Stalin awarded Frank
Pick, LT's chief executive, an Honorary Badge of Merit. Gants
Hill, which opened in 1947, earned itself a Festival of Britain
Award for Architectural Merit in 1951.

13. (b) Paolozzi was also responsible for 'Piscator', the sculpture
that sits in the forecourt of Euston Station.

14. (a) On 11 June 1939, the St. John's Wood station on the
Metropolitan line near the famous cricket ground was renamed
Lord's Station. Unfortunately, the extension of the Bakerloo (now
Jubilee) line to Stanmore that November resulted in the creation
of another station serving St. John's Wood. During the war, the
Lord's Station was closed and never reopened.

15. (c) The Queen travelled the seventeen miles into London
from Slough at forty-four miles per hour, a speed Prince Albert
complained to the conductor was too fast.

16. (b) To gain the coveted Green Badge that allows them to
work anywhere in Greater London, all cabbies must learn 320
routes. It can take between two and four years to pass The
Knowledge. The drivers are quizzed on the various landmarks
and places of interest on each of these routes and are expected
to show a detailed knowledge of the city as a whole. They must

also prove that they are temperamentally suited to dealir.
the public and the stresses of the job.

17. (c) In 2006, the then-mayor of London, Ken Livingstone, caused a diplomatic row when he called the U.S. Ambassador a 'chiseling little crook' for refusing the pay the charge. The Embassy maintained that the charge was a tax, which cannot be levied on foreign envoys, while Transport for London argued it was a road 'toll' of the type British diplomats are required to pay in the U.S.

18. (b) The Barbadian government, battling with severe unemployment, had initially approached London Transport with the idea. The scheme was extended to Malta, Jamaica and Trinidad in the 1960s and lasted until 1970. It played its own small part in making London the great multicultural capital that it is today.

19. (a) In 1929, 55 Broadway, constructed above St. James's tube station, was the tallest office building in London. Epstein's figures, a male and female nude, above the main entrances, proved so controversial that Frank Pick offered his resignation. It was not accepted and the furore eventually died down.

20. (c) Following the King's Cross station fire, in which thirty-one people died, London Underground banned smoking across its entire network in 1987. But until 1991, smokers could still spark up on the upper decks of London buses. A ban on alcohol on London's transport system came into force on the 1 June 2008.

JEWISH LONDON

The area they lived in is known as Old Jewry.

.. (b) Richard had barred all Jews from attending his coronation. A small group, however, attempted to present gifts to the new king, and were attacked by an angry mob convinced the King had ordered them to murder any Jews in the vicinity. The King belatedly issued a writ asking for the Jews to be left alone and had one of the perpetrators punished. But anti-Semitic violence continued for the rest of Richard's reign.

3. (a) In 1655, Menasseh ben Israel, a prominent Dutch rabbi, and six Jews living covertly in London, had sent a petition to Oliver Cromwell asking for permission to conduct religious services in their homes. The following year, Cromwell invited Menasseh ben Israel to London to negotiate the readmission of the Jews to England. The majority of the first to settle were Sephardic Jews from Holland who had descended from those expelled from Spain and Portugal in 1492; a small community of twenty or so Marrano families established the synagogue in Creechurch Lane. Pepys paid a visit to it on 14 October 1663 but was rather perplexed by the services, declaring, 'I never did see so much, or could have imagined there had been any religion in the whole world so absurdly performed as this'. A plaque on the Cunard Building on the corner of Creechurch Lane and Bury Street commemorates the site.

4. (b) This roof was destroyed by fire in 1738, and replaced in 1749. The roof and the building were again damaged in the IRA bombing campaigns in the City of London in 1992 and 1993.

5. (b) Dedicated to the more than six million Jews who were

murdered by the Nazis, the garden consists of two boulc
set in raked gravel and surrounded by silver birch trees. Ar
inscription reads: 'For these I weep. Streams of tears flow fro.
my eyes because of the destruction of my people'. It was create
in 1983 by the architect Richard Seifert, perhaps best known for
the Centre Point Tower on New Oxford Street.

6. (b) Levy was a printer with premises on Shoe Lane off
Fleet Street and the proprietor of the *Sunday Times*. In 1855 he
founded the *Daily Telegraph*, pricing it at just a penny—the *Times*
at that point cost seven pence—putting 'a first class newspaper',
as he stated, 'within the reach of Everyman'. The paper was
launched under the slogan, 'the largest, best, and cheapest
newspaper in the world' and was outselling the *Times* within just
a few months.

7. (c) Joseph Avis signed a contract to put up a synagogue for
£2,750 but refused to take his fee when it was finished, because
he decided that it was wrong to profit from building a house of
God.

8. (a) Edward VII

9. (b) Gertler was a pacifist and the picture, painted in 1916, was
intended as a damning indictment of the First World War. In a
letter to the artist, D. H. Lawrence wrote: 'It is the best modern
picture I have seen'. Gertler is buried in Willesden Jewish
Cemetery.

10. (b) Katz lasted until the late 1990s. Today his name is
preserved on the front of 92 Brick Lane but the shop is currently
a venue for art installations.

dinsky was the shammes or caretaker of this former
gue. His old room at the top of the building was
vered by workmen in the 1970s, immaculately, if eerily,
served. A calendar from 1963, when the synagogue closed as
place of worship, and books and newspapers were found laid
out on a table, leading many to suppose that he'd been spirited
away in mysterious not to say supernatural circumstances.
The reality, unearthed by the artist Rachel Lichtenstein and
the writer Iain Sinclair, proved less occult. Rodinsky had died of
bronchial pneumonia in a mental institution in Surrey in 1969.

12. (a) Sir Oswald Mosley, the leader of the British Union of
Fascists, had intended to march through the heart of the Jewish
End. But in what subsequently was dubbed 'the battle of Cable
Street', local residents and antifascist campaigners stymied his
attempts to enter the area. Mosley and his "black shirts" were
forced to retreat under a police escort.

13. (c) Hasidic Jews seeking to escape the crowded tenements
of the old East End first made this northeastern suburb their
home in the late nineteenth century. The New Synagogue first
established on Leadenhall Street in 1769 before moving to Great
Helen's in 1838, has been based on Egerton Road in Stamford
Hill since 1915.

14. (b) Ivy House on North End Road was the London residence
of the Russian ballet dancer until her death in 1931. For some
time after that the building was owned by the Industrial
Orthopaedic Society and served as an out-patient department
to Manor House Hospital.

15. (a) Disraeli's father had him baptized at the age of thirteen

after resigning from the Bevis Marks Synagogue following
quarrel. This bronze statue by Mario Raggi was unveiled in
on the second anniversary of the statesman and novelist's de

16. (a) Basevi was a pupil of Sir John Soane and Disraeli's cousin.
He met an untimely death in 1845, when he fell off the roof of Ely
Cathedral in Cambridgeshire while inspecting some repairs.

17. (c) Morris Bloom opened his first kosher restaurant on
Brick Lane in 1920. The restaurant moved to Whitechapel High
Street in 1952 and was a magnet for City traders, stallholders
and celebrities. Israeli prime minister Golda Meir and Princess
Margaret were among those who stopped by to enjoy its
chopped liver, lokshen soup and cholent. Bloom's may have left
the East End, but a second restaurant opened in Golders Green
in 1965 and, in 2007 a further branch in Edgware, to keep the
tradition alive.

18. (b) Minnie Lansbury (born Glassman) died from pneumonia
in 1922 aged thirty-two. Her husband, Edgar, was the son of East
End politician and Labour Party leader George Lansbury. Edgar
later remarried. His second wife had been on the stage, and
their daughter, Angela Lansbury, was to follow in her mother's
footsteps.

19. (a) Born in Aldgate in 1764, Mendoza pioneered the art of
defensive boxing and was the first boxer to have a royal patron,
some of his bouts being sponsored by the Prince of Wales.

20. (b) Member of the Crazy Gang and half of the comic singing
duo, Flanagan and Allen, Flanagan was born Reuben Weintrop
and attended the Jews Free School on Bell Lane.

LONDON FIRSTS

Roller skates were first demonstrated in Soho Square, London, in 1760 at a masquerade party given by the then famous hostess, Mrs. Cornelys. The clock maker and instrument maker John Joseph Merlin made his appearance at the party gliding across the floor on boots that he had adapted by fitting them with wheels. Unfortunately he had failed to devise any method of stopping himself and he crashed into a large mirror.

2. (c) Archer, the son of an Irish mother and a Barbadian father, ran a photographic business in Battersea Park Road. He became an active participant in the politics of the neighbourhood and was elected as the Mayor of Battersea after many years as a local councillor.

3. (b) The Scotsman John Logie Baird began his research into the transmission of visual images in Hastings in the early 1920s but moved to London in 1924. He rented an attic room at 22 Frith Street, Soho, to use as a workshop, and it was there on 26 January 1926 that members of the Royal Institution made up the first television audience. The room was above what is now Bar Italia.

4. (a) On 4 September 1917, during the First World War, a bomb was dropped very close to Cleopatra's Needle during a Zeppelin air raid. The damage it did can still be clearly seen on the pedestal of the Sphinx which is part of the monument.

5. (c) The Hindostanee Coffee House opened off Portman Square in 1810. Its owner was a man called Dean Mahomed. His establishment offered, in the words of one of its advertisements, 'India dishes in the highest perfection' but, sadly, the public wasn't ready for them and the Hindostanee went bust in 1812.

6. (c) John Flamsteed was the first Astronomer Royal, a̧
by Charles II in 1675. Flamsteed House, the oldest part of ̧
Royal Observatory at Greenwich, was built by Sir Christophe̱
Wren.

7. (b) London's first traffic island was constructed in St. James's
Street in 1864 at the personal expense of a Colonel Pierpoint,
who was afraid of being run over on his way to his Pall Mall club.
When it was finished, he dashed across the road to admire his
creation and was knocked down by a cab.

8. (b) In 1634 a retired mariner named Captain Bailey placed
four hackney coaches for hire at the Maypole in the Strand
which is where St. Mary's Church now stands.

9. (c) The so-called fourth plinth, situated in the northwest
corner of the square, was erected in 1841 and was intended
to support an equestrian statue of William IV that never
materialised. Since 1999, it has been used as the site for
contemporary art works of which Mark Wallinger's was the first.
In 2009, for a hundred consecutive days, 2,400 members of the
public were given an hour each on the plinth to do more or less
exactly what they wanted.

10. (a) Built by J. R. Whitley on the site of what is now Earl's
Court Exhibition Centre, the giant wheel had a diameter of 300
feet and was opened to the public in July 1895. It was closed and
demolished in 1907.

11. (b) As well as building both telescopes and microscopes,
Ayscough experimented with tinted lenses in spectacles. His
glasses were intended to correct problems of vision rather than

...ne eyes from the sun but they were, in effect, the first sunglasses.

(c) A rare migrant to Britain from the European mainland, ...is butterfly was given the name Camberwell Beauty in the eighteenth century after two specimens were caught in Coldharbour Lane, Camberwell.

13. (a) All three men escaped from the Tower but the first to do so was Flambard who was the political right-hand man to William Rufus, King of England between 1087 and 1100. He was arrested when Henry I succeeded to the throne. Flambard plied his guards with drink, rendering them unconscious, and escaped by letting a rope down from a window.

14. (c) Designed by an engineer named John Peake Knight, they were based on the same principle as railway signals and consisted of a revolving lantern with red and green lights. Only months after the installation, the lights, powered by gas, exploded and seriously injured the policeman who was operating them.

15. (c) Sitting in a room at Brown's, Alexander Graham Bell made a call to the family home of the hotel's owner in Ravenscourt Park.

16. (b) The first coffeehouse was opened in St. Michael's Alley in 1652 by a native of Smyrna called Pasqua Rosee who had arrived in the city as servant to a merchant returning from Turkey.

17. (a) Hiram Maxim was an American who moved to London, opened a workshop in Hatton Gardens and eventually became a

naturalised Briton and a knight of the realm. His Maxim C
the first fully automatic machine gun.

18. (c) Vauxhall Gardens was a pleasure garden in Kennington on the south bank of the Thames from the seventeenth century until the middle of the nineteenth century. Cocking's parachute jump was the main attraction on a Grand Fete Day in July 1837 but it went terribly wrong from the start and several thousand people saw him falling to his death. His body was eventually found some miles away in a field near the village of Lee.

19. (a) Between 1892 and 1894, Bremer drove his car several times along the streets of Walthamstow, although he usually chose to take his invention out after dark to avoid startling the neighbours and attracting unwelcome attention from the police. The Bremer car, which was still sufficiently roadworthy to complete the London to Brighton Run in 1964, is on display in the Vestry House museum in Walthamstow.

20. (b) When an elderly shopkeeper was killed at Chapman's Oil and Colour Shop in Deptford High Street on 27 March 1905, one of the few clues to the murderer was a thumb mark left on an emptied cash box. Using the new technique of fingerprints, it was identified as belonging to one Alfred Stratton and he and his brother Albert were eventually convicted of the crime.

LOST LONDON

1. (a) Marble Arch was originally built by the architect John Nash on The Mall as a gateway to the newly refurbished Buckingham Palace but was moved to its present site in the year of the Great Exhibition.

ppendale and his sons had their business at the
tin's Lane site for more than six decades. Reynolds's
o was in Leicester Square and Paul de Lamerie, the
g's silversmith in the reign of the first two Georges, had
is workshop in Gerrard Street. All three sites are marked by
plaques.

3. (b) Built in Piccadilly in 1812, with a facade that supposedly
was in the form of an ancient Egyptian temple, the hall was one
of the chief venues for exhibitions and entertainments in the city
throughout most of the nineteenth century. It was demolished in
1905 and an office block, now called Egyptian House, was built
on the site.

4. (c) Gamages was a maze of interconnecting rooms and
buildings in which it was said that you could buy anything
cheaper than anywhere else in London. It closed in 1972. Swan &
Edgar stood on the corner of Regent Street and Piccadilly Circus
from the early decades of the nineteenth century until 1982. Bon
Marché, the first purpose-built department store in London, was
in Brixton Road. The building can still be seen although the shop
has long gone.

5. (b) The roars of the lions and the tigers could be heard in the
street outside and often frightened horses.

6. (c) The Marshalsea was closed in 1842, more than a decade
before Dickens published *Little Dorrit*, but the novelist knew
the prison from his childhood in the 1820s when his father was
imprisoned there for debt. All that remains of it is a small section
of wall marked by a plaque.

7. (a) A futuristic, cigar-shaped sculpture with, as people joked at the time, 'no visible means of support', the Skylon was constructed as part of the Festival of Britain in 1951. It was dismantled the following year.

8. (b) The Royal Aquarium, a Victorian palace of entertainment which included an art gallery, a skating rink and a theatre as well as tanks of sea creatures, stood there from the 1870s to the end of the nineteenth century.

9. (b) The spectators at the course stood on the sides of the hill and watched the horses race around a circuit around its base. The street name of Hippodrome Place is a reminder of it.

10. (c) The Blackfriars Barge dates from the second century AD and sank in the Thames while carrying a cargo of stone for use in building work.

11. (a) The original entrance to Euston station, designed by Sir Philip Hardwick and inspired by the Roman architecture he had seen on his travels in Italy, was erected in 1837. Despite a campaign to save it, led by the poet John Betjeman, it was knocked down in 1962.

12. (b) Wyld was a cartographer and MP. His Great Globe, which stood in Leicester Square from 1851 to 1862, was his most ambitious attempt to educate the public in the geography of the world. Within a purpose-built pavilion was a hollow globe, sixty feet in diameter. Visitors climbed staircases within the globe and stood on platforms to view scale models of seas, continents, mountain ranges, etc.

was at Hercules Buildings that a friend found Blake and sitting naked in the garden, reading *Paradise Lost*. When end tried to retire, the painter and poet is said to have ed out, 'Come in, come in! It is only Adam and Eve, you know!'

14. (c) Although critics might well have claimed that it resembled both a brothel and a place of worship, the Temple of Health and Hymen was essentially a clinic, established in 1781 by a persuasive and charming quack doctor named James Graham to help those suffering from marital problems and infertility. Emma Hart, later to become Nelson's mistress Lady Hamilton, worked there as a young woman.

15. (a) The correct attire for gentlemen attending Almack's was knee breeches.

16. (a) Soyer bought Gore House, a mansion which stood where the Royal Albert Hall now stands, and attempted to interest Londoners in the delights of fine eating. Extravagantly furnished, themed rooms with names like 'La Grotte des Neiges Eternelles' and 'La Chambre Ardante D'Apollo' were intended to pull in the customers. The venture was a disaster, losing Soyer £7000 in five months, and it soon closed.

17. (b) Charles Jamrach ran a business importing such animals for zoos and circuses. At the north entrance to Tobacco Dock, Wapping, there is a statue of a small boy in front of a tiger. This records an incident in which a fully grown Bengal tiger escaped from Jamrach's and began to make its way down the Commercial Road. The large cat seized a small child in its mouth but was eventually persuaded by Carl Jamrach himself to release the boy unharmed.

18. (a) A buttress from the old prison can still be seen ⸱
river opposite Tate Britain. An inscription on it reminds p⸱
by that it once stood at the head of the steps from which m⸱
prisoners sentenced to transportation to the colonies embark⸱
on their journey to Australia.

19. (c) Known as Whittington's Longhouse, it could seat dozens
of people seeking relief and was flushed clear of filth regularly by
the incoming and outgoing of the tide.

20. (a) The Steelyard, which took its name from the German
word *stahlhof*, was where the merchants of the great trading
enterprise known as the Hanseatic League had its headquarters.

LONDON MEN AND WOMEN

1. (b) Wilkes genuinely was cross-eyed as can be seen in
contemporary portraits of him. The statue of the philanthropist
Sir Sydney Waterlow in Waterlow Park, Highgate, depicts him
leaning on his umbrella.

2. (a) Born in Switzerland, Marie Grosholtz is better known as
Madame Tussaud. The first permanent London home for her
waxwork exhibition was in Baker Street. Madame Tussauds
moved to its present site in the Marylebone Road in 1884, more
than thirty years after its founder's death.

3. (b) All three men were doctors at the hospital in the
nineteenth century.

ah Siddons. The statue, which is close to her grave,
veiled by Sir Henry Irving in 1897.

c) Ben Pimlico was supposedly a publican famous for his
nut-brown ale'.

6. (a) Ada, a highly gifted mathematician, engaged in long
correspondence with Charles Babbage and clearly saw the
possibilities of his calculating machines. She wrote a paper in
1843 in which she predicted their use in the creation of graphics
and music. The computing language ADA is named in her
honour.

7. (b) In the 1870s and 1880s, Grossmith created many of the
most famous of the Gilbert and Sullivan roles including the
aesthetic poet Reginald Bunthorne in *Patience* and Ko-Ko, the
reluctant Lord High Executioner, in *The Mikado*.

8. (c) Poe's foster parents brought him to London when he
was a small boy and he attended Manor House School in Stoke
Newington, which he described in later life as 'a misty looking
village of England'.

9. (b) Horniman's Tea provided the money for the museum but
Frederick John was the driving force behind what remains an
extraordinary, eclectic collection of everything from Ancient
Egyptian musical instruments to a stuffed walrus from the
Canadian Arctic.

10. (a) Lilian Baylis turned the Old Vic into one of the great
London theatres, famous for its productions of Shakespeare. She
also supervised the reopening of Sadler's Wells in 1931.

11. (c) In his own words, Leno 'came into the world a mer
in Agar Town in 1860. Edward VII enjoyed his comedy so r
that he invited Leno to perform for him at Sandringham.

12. (b) Phoebe Hessel, born in Stepney in 1713, disguised herself
as a man and served in the British army in Europe and the West
Indies. She became a celebrity when her story was revealed and
lived to a great old age. Two streets in Stepney (Amazon Street
and Hessel Street) derive their names from her.

13. (a) Born in 1669, Susanna Annesley married Samuel Wesley
in 1690 and bore him seventeen children including John, the
father of Methodism, and Charles, the hymn writer.

14. (a) Newton became Master of the Royal Mint, which was
then situated within the Tower of London, in 1700, and remained
in the post until he died in 1727.

15. (c) It was during his short stay in Upper Wimpole Street,
which lasted only a few months, that Doyle sent 'A Scandal in
Bohemia', the first of the Sherlock Holmes short stories, to his
literary agent.

16. (c) Pepys was the only one of the three who was actually
born in London. Although they both became famous adopted
sons of the city, Dr. Johnson was born in Lichfield and Dickens in
Portsmouth.

17. (b) The creators of Philip Marlowe, Jeeves and Wooster and
Captain Hornblower may seem to have little immediately in
common but they were all educated at Dulwich.

...e typical summer drink of the English upper middle ... was created by a man named James Pimm. Pimm ...ally thought that his concoction would be used as a ...estive tonic but his customers soon decided that it was best ...runk as a cocktail.

19. (b) Gustavus Vassa or Olaudah Equiano was born on the west coast of Africa and taken as a slave to the West Indies when he was ten. He gained his freedom and came to London as a young man. He was the author of a book about his experiences and a campaigner against the slave trade.

20. (a) Gompers grew up to become a major figure in the history of the American labour movement and has everything from parks to schools named after him in the U.S. The USS *Samuel Gompers* was in service from 1967 to 1985.

THE LONDON DEAD

1. (a) He is supposed to have told the Dean of Westminster that 'six feet long by two feet wide is too much for me: two feet by two feet will do for all I want'.

2. (b) Braidwood was killed when a wall collapsed on him. The Tooley Street fire, which began in a riverside warehouse, was one of the worst blazes in London during the nineteenth century. It took two days to bring under control and the ruins continued to smoulder for a fortnight.

3. (a) Bloody Sunday was a demonstration against government policy in Ireland. Linnell was a Socialist clerk who was killed during clashes between the demonstrators, who included such famous names as William Morris and George Bernard Shaw, and mounted police.

4. (c) Perhaps the best known cemetery in London, Highgate is the final home for many famous people, including Karl Marx, the Victorian novelist George Eliot, the scientist Michael Faraday, the movie pioneer William Friese-Greene and the author of *The Hitchhiker's Guide to the Galaxy*, Douglas Adams.

5. (a) The Dogs' Cemetery, which hides away behind the old gatekeeper's cottage at Victoria Gate at a point where Hyde Park and Kensington Gardens meet, began in the nineteenth century when the Duchess of Cambridge was looking for somewhere to lay to rest a beloved pet.

6. (a) Markov was a dissident Bulgarian writer and broadcaster. A passing pedestrian, assumed to be a member of the Bulgarian secret services jabbed him in the back of the leg as he stood at the bus stop. A pellet containing the poison ricin had been fired into him and he died three days later.

7. (c) Thomas Parr was supposedly born in 1483 and lived through the reigns of ten monarchs, from Edward IV to Charles I. A Shropshire man, he was brought to London as a curiosity in 1635. The shock was too much for him and he died a few weeks after arriving. The king ordered that he should be buried in the Abbey.

8. (b) Briggs had been attacked by a German tailor living in London named Franz Müller. Although Müller fled to New York, a jeweller in Cheapside (called, rather bizarrely, John Death) had identified him from a photograph as the man who had sold him a gold chain belonging to Briggs. He was extradited, tried, found guilty and hanged.

9. (a) Ducrow, an equestrian performer who was the proprietor of the famous Astley's Amphitheatre in the middle of the nineteenth century, has one of the most elaborate of all the mausoleums in Kensal Green Cemetery. It was originally painted in bright colours but these have since faded.

10. (a) 'The mair mischief, the mair sport', Lovat is reported to have said as he watched the stand collapse.

11. (c) Chung Ling Soo's most famous trick saw him standing in front of assistants who seemed to fire bullets at him. He appeared to catch them in his mouth and spit them out onto a plate. On this night, the planning went fatally wrong and a real bullet struck him in the chest.

12. (a) Several hundred people were gathered in an upper room of the house to take part in a religious service when the floor beams gave way and large numbers of the congregation were plunged into the room below.

13. (c) In 1839, workmen excavating under the chancel of the church of St. James Garlickhythe came across a medieval mummy. Known as Jimmy Garlick, this rare example of natural mummification was on display in a glass case in the church for many years but is no longer on public view.

14. (a) On that date a huge vat burst its hoops in the Horseshoe Brewery in Tottenham Court Road. This ruptured other vats and eventually more than a million litres of beer swept through the brewery walls and into the streets. The sea of beer carried away neighbouring houses and drowned eight people. The site of the Horseshoe Brewery is now occupied by the Dominion Theatre.

15. (c) Josef Jakobs had been parachuted into southern England in July 1941. He injured himself on landing and was soon captured. He was executed by firing squad on a miniature rifle range in the King's House in the Tower. Carl Lody was executed in November 1914. Henry Laurens, the only American ever imprisoned in the Tower, was there between 1779 and 1781 but was eventually released.

16. (a) The Hebrew Dramatic Club on what was then called Princes Street also housed a library and a restaurant. On the night of 18 January 1887, when a popular operetta called 'The Gypsy Girl' was being performed, a member of the audience yelled 'Fire!' causing a rush for the exits. Seventeen people died in the ensuing melee. It closed shortly afterwards.

17. (c) Sir Richard Burton. The eye-catching memorial to Burton, who was a linguist, explorer and the translator of such risqué works of literature as the *Kama Sutra* and *The Arabian Nights*, is twelve feet by eleven feet and presents an unusual sight in a suburban London burial ground.

18. (c) Halliwell shared the flat with Orton but had been unable to deal with his lover's growing success as the author of black comedies like *Loot* and *Entertaining Mr. Sloane*. He was also jealous of Orton's adventurous and promiscuous sex life. After murdering him, Halliwell committed suicide by swallowing twenty-two Nembutal pills washed down with the juice from a tin of grapefruit.

19. (a) Like many of his contemporaries, the artist George Frederick Watts was much moved by the story of Alice Ayres. Watts thought that such people should be remembered and lobbied for a memorial to them. The Memorial to Heroic Self-Sacrifice was unveiled in Postman's Park in July 1900 and now consists of some fifty plaques recording the deeds of those who died saving others.

20. (b) When the philosopher Jeremy Bentham died in 1832, he left most of his estate to what is now University College, London. He also left the college his body. In accordance with his belief that the dead should be useful to the living, he instructed his medical friends at the university to use it as a means of illustrating a series of lectures. Once the lectures were over, his corpse was to be dressed in the clothes that he usually wore and placed on perpetual display. He was to become the first example of what he called an 'auto-icon'. He still sits in the college in a large case with a plate-glass front, wearing the clothes he used to put on, and with his stick in his hand. A wax head has replaced his own, which is preserved in a mummified state in a box nearby.

A LONDON MISCELLANY

1. (a) This was the first time this had happened in the 1,500-year history of the sport. Most of the wrestlers stayed at the nearby Royal Garden Hotel where the management was obliged to undertake some modifications of the rooms to cope with the arrival of a phalanx of huge Asians. Beds and chairs were reinforced and the showers, which had sprays too small to send water to the farthest reaches of the wrestlers' bodies, were adapted.

2. (c) Civet cats produce a strong-smelling secretion used in the perfume industry then and now. Before he achieved fame as a writer, Defoe struggled to make money in a number of ventures of which breeding civets was the least likely and the least successful.

3. (b) Lenin stayed briefly at Percy Circus off the Pentonville Road when he was attending the Third Congress of the Russian Social Democratic Party, held in London.

4. (b) Phyllis Pearsall compiled the first edition of the *A-Z* in the 1930s. She rose at five in the morning each day and walked eighteen miles through the streets, taking notes, eventually completing 23,000 individual street entries which she kept in shoeboxes under her bed. No publisher was interested so she published it herself, delivering copies to branches of W. H. Smith in a wheelbarrow. By the time of her death in 1996, the *A-Z* had sold millions of copies.

5. (a) Fourteen of the stonemasons who had worked on the construction of the column ate a meal on the platform at its top just before the statue of the admiral was placed on it. The large model of a dinosaur was the setting for a dinner eleven years earlier. The reconstruction of an iguanodon, together with others, can still be seen today. Marc Brunel's tunnel under the Thames was used for a banquet for 150 people in 1827.

6. (b) Lord Noel-Buxton believed that the Romans under Julius Caesar had crossed the Thames by a ford at this point and was trying to prove his case. He was obliged to give up his attempt when the water rose to his neck and showed every sign that it was going to continue to rise.

7. (b) Once rejoicing in the even longer name of 'I Am the Only Running Footman', this historic pub provided a title for the American crime writer Martha Grimes who has produced a series of books under titles taken from the names of old British pubs.

8. (a) The Great Smog of 1952 was the worst of the twentieth century. As fog, coal fire smoke and industrial emissions combined, visibility in the city was reduced to inches rather than feet and several thousand people died of bronchial and cardiovascular illnesses made worse by the smog.

9. (b) The statue of Shackleton is by Charles Jagger, a sculptor best known for his figures on war memorials, including the bronze of the soldier reading a letter from home in Paddington Station.

10. (b) Commissioned by Frank Pick, the man in charge of the Underground at the time, and designed by the well-known typographer and calligrapher Edward Johnston, the font was first used in 1916.

11. (a) Martin was then in his seventies and had a long history of commitment to radical causes. He had also fought in countless duels and part of his concern for the welfare of animals seemed to originate in the fact that they couldn't defend themselves or their honour by calling out their tormentors. 'Sir, an ox cannot hold a pistol', he once said to someone who questioned the need for legislation to protect animals. The Royal Humane Society was founded in another coffee house (in St. Paul's churchyard) in the 1770s. The Metropolitan Free Drinking Fountain Association was established in 1859.

12. (b) In 1619 the Mortlake Tapestry Works were established by the Thames on land once owned by the famous mathematician, astrologer and alchemist John Dee. For the rest of the century, it produced some of the finest tapestries in Europe.

13. (c) A monument to the history of immigration and religious variety in the area, it began life as a Huguenot chapel in 1742. In 1898 it became the Spitalfields Great Synagogue and was converted into a mosque in the 1980s.

14. (a) It is owned by Dulwich College, the nearby public school. The old board showing the tolls, which dates from the end of the eighteenth century, is still there. Taking a flock of sheep through the gate costs 2d. Pedestrians can pass through it for free.

15. (b) His main claim to fame is that he invented the 'closed' diving helmet which allowed a diver to stay under water longer than any previous equipment. The Denmark Street workshop was where Siebe, who won several medals for his inventions at the 1851 Great Exhibition, also created other machines including a weighing machine and one for making ice. Luke Howard, who has a blue plaque to his name in Bruce Grove, Tottenham, classified the clouds; Gus Elen, remembered in Thurleigh Avenue, Balham, was the music hall singer.

16. (a) (b) and **(c)** All three, according to a contemporary magazine article about the place.

17. (b) All three groups were basically gangs of violent upper-class thugs. The Mohocks, who took their name from the Mohawk Indians in North America, terrorised the streets and were particularly renowned for stuffing their victims in wooden barrels and rolling them down Snow Hill near Smithfield Market.

18. (c) Pickering Place is a tiny courtyard at the end of an alleyway running along the side of the wine merchants Berry Brothers and Rudd. Britain was one of the first nations to recognise the Republic of Texas when it broke away from Mexico in the 1830s. The plaque records that, 'In this building was the legation for the ministers from the Republic of Texas to the Court of St. James 1842–1845'. The Texan Republic ended when the state became the twenty-eighth in the United States.

19. (b) There are several different theories why Russians use **Вокзал** (vokzal) as one of their words for a railway station. One suggestion is that a group of early Russian railway builders visited the area in the 1840s, saw the name on the station and mistook it for the general word for that type of building. The most likely explanation, however, is that Russians had already borrowed the word from Vauxhall Pleasure Gardens to describe an amusement park by the early 1800s. The very first railway in Russia ran from St. Petersburg to just such a 'vokzal' and the name was then transferred to any railway terminus.

20. (a) When Charles II was restored to the English throne in 1660, Cromwell's body was disinterred from its tomb in Westminster Abbey and was given a posthumous execution at Tyburn. His head was then placed on a long spike on the roof of Westminster Hall. There it remained for more than four decades until the violent winds of the Great Storm dislodged it.

ABOUT THE AUTHORS

A former bookseller and website editor, **Travis Elborough** has been a freelance writer, author and cultural commentator for the last decade. His books include *The Bus We Loved: London's Affair with the Routemaster* and *The Long-Player Goodbye: the Album from Vinyl to iPod and Back Again* (published in the U.S. as *The Vinyl Countdown*). He is a regular contributor to *The Guardian* and has written for *The Sunday Times*, *New Statesman*, *The Oldie*, *TATE ETC.* and *BBC History* magazine and frequently appears on *BBC Radio 4* and *Five Live*. He lives in London.

Nick Rennison has worked as a writer, editor and bookseller for more than twenty years. He has a particular interest in London's history and literature and has written extensively on both subjects. His *London Blue Plaque Guide* has been through three editions in the last decade and he has also published *The Book of London Lists*, described by the *London Evening Standard* as a book that 'can teach even the most die-hard Londoner something they didn't know'. His many other books include *Sherlock Holmes: The Unauthorised Biography*, *The Rivals of Sherlock Holmes*, *The Good Reading Guide to Crime Fiction* and *Roget: The Man Who Became a Book*. He is currently working on a crime novel set in nineteenth-century London.